A SPECIAL CALLING

*A Biography of
The Reverend Lud Flanigan*

JIMMIE L CLAY
MHA, FACHE

iUniverse, Inc.
New York   Bloomington

iUniverse books may be ordered through booksellers or by contacting·

iUniverse
1663 Liberty Drive
Bloomington, IN 47403
www.iuniverse.com
1-800-Authors (1-800-288-4677)

ISBN: 978-1-4502-2073-6 (sc)
ISBN: 978-1-4502-2074-3 (ebook)

Printed in the United States of America

iUniverse rev. date: 03/12/2010

DEDICATION

We dedicate this book in memory and recognition to the late Dollie Short Flanigan who was born in Pelican of DeSoto Parish, Louisiana.

Dollie attended Mount Olive School where she met Lud Flanigan in the late 1930s. She also attained additional education at DeSoto Parish Training School in Mansfield, LA.

Dollie and the Reverend Lud Flanigan were married for 63 years and eleven months and reared three sons to adulthood together prior to her passing to eternal life on September 8, 2003.

Mrs. Dollie Flanigan was more than the statement implies, "Behind every great man, there is a great woman." First, she accepted Christ early in life and became a devoted church member before marriage. She continued this devotion after marriage by creating and sustaining a faithful, loyal, and supportive spousal relationship until her passing. Secondly and most significant is the fact that she was not only recognized as the "First Lady" of the twelve churches where her husband was pastor, but served above this capacity faithfully with him on a daily basis. Members of the various churches noticed this devotion in the very beginning of her husband's ministry. Such services within the church included being a member of Deaconess and other church organizations as well as serving as an advisor.

Mrs. Flanigan never sought recognition for services rendered within any of the churches where her husband was pastor for more than sixty years nor did she desired to be recognized at the church where she called home, the Mount Olive Baptist Church of Mansfield, LA. However, she received numerous tributes and acknowledgments as a devoted Christian woman who went about her services in a model but quiet way influencing others. At its thirty-eighth anniversary on August 8, 1993, the Paradise Baptist Church paid tribute to Mrs. Flanigan. In parts, the acknowledgement stated, "Sister

Flanigan, like her husband, has been a pillar in the growth and service to God of the Paradise Baptist Church. She has been a willing worker in the church, a mother, advisor, and an extension of the pastor as they have served here with meaning and purpose and with true Christian dedication." The church, again at its Forty-Seventh anniversary on August 11, 2002, paid special tribute to Mrs. Flanigan. The church membership honored her by saying; "Sister Flanigan has been pastor Flanigan's wife for 63 years. She has been steadfast in her role as the church's First Lady and has served well in numerous capacities. Over the years, she has provided support and leadership in various church departments and her leadership has been well accepted and appreciated. She has exemplified true Christian character and her familiar face is synonymous with all things Paradise. Sister Flanigan's role has been characterized by quiet dignity and by example. Paradise has been blessed to have such a Christian woman to serve as its First Lady." Unquestionably, she has embodied Christ in her actions and deeds and reflected HIM in every aspect of her individual, family and religious life.

ACKNOWLEDGMENTS

Reverend Lud Flanigan and I want to thank and express our sincere appreciation to those who were invaluable resources in the preparation of this book. These individuals include the 16 people (and family members of those deceased) who are featured under "Reflections of Greatness and Spotlights on Legacy." All sixteen distinguished individuals are featured in their own uniqueness and the exceptional contributions they made while working at the schools and/or the accomplishments after graduating from DeSoto Parish Training School and/or DeSoto High School.

We are most grateful to Nathaniel Lilly, Phoebia J. Bennett, James W. Cummings, Norvella Goree Whitaker, Louis C. Wells, Sr., Mayor Curtis McCoy, Myrtle R. Turner, Loree J. Washington, Wilbur T. Purvis, the granddaughter, Tonya G. Washington, and the sons; Louis, Wilbert and Roosevelt for taking time to provide memorable remarks that have been written under section, "I Remember The Reverend Lud Flanigan." This section is one of the highlights of this book because of the fact that each person recognized therein expressed his/her own personal feelings, observations, and relationship with Reverend Flanigan. As a result of the expressions, the reader is in for a pleasurable experience from the first expression until the last...and wished there was more.

A special thanks and recognition of a debt that cannot be ever paid are extended to Louis Flanigan, the eldest son of the Reverend Lud Flanigan. An authentic manuscript for this book would not have been possible without the gracious input of Louis. His unwavering support and advice throughout the development of the manuscript made every section therein complete. A vast majority of the information written relating to the histories of DeSoto Parish School System for African-Americans, and the Reverend Flanigan's life and career as a minister and the churches' events, came from documentations created by Louis. The accumulation and transformation of most of the information shown under "Reflections of Greatness and Spotlights on Legacy" were generated from the work of Louis Flanigan.

I want to thank a close friend and colleague, R. Larry Fullwood, Director Department of Veterans Affairs, Retired, BA, MSW, MPH. Larry took the time to review the entire manuscript and suggested how it could be rearranged to make it easier to read and enhance the flow of information about the featured person. Other noteworthy people who contributed greatly to the completion of the manuscript by editing each page for possible errors, etc. include Dorothy Kennedy, former Executive Secretary and Public Affairs Assistant; Rudolph Washington, colleague, and retired school principal; and Lisea Johnson, former Hospital Administrative Resident, Recruitment & Development Specialist.

Needless to say there is a long list of people that have helped to make this book a great success and worthwhile to read, that extends well beyond those mentioned, to whom again we say…thank you so much for your devoted assistance.

In order for me to provide viable insight on the brain, memory processes and other important related topics, serious research and reflection were required. There is no substitute for time spent on reading and reviewing the information collected on these subjects. Some of the information and genuine facts were taken from certain websites on the Internet whereas others were found in textbooks at various libraries. All of the resources are recognized in the references section of this book.

INTRODUCTION

A Special Calling is a biography of the Reverend Lud Flanigan. This is a true story of a retired Baptist minister who without breaking stride, quietly glided past the age of ninety (90) while the manuscript for his biography was still in it's planning stages. Throughout his life, the Reverend Lud Flanigan has been recognized to possess an exceptional good memory. However, his ability to retain and recall information and events that occurred several years in the past, which most people forget within hours or days, became more pronounced after he reached his eighties. Undoubtedly, a superb memory enabled him to accrue an exceptional career as a minister as well as an outstanding citizen within the community where he lived.

Reverend Flanigan learned early in life, perhaps sooner than most others that our destiny is fashioned by what all of us do, by prayers, good or not so good deeds and desires of each person he met. As a parallel, one word typed on a page in this book, one after another ultimately makes a sentence, a paragraph, a chapter and finally an entire book. The activity for a pastor of a church is probably the highest responsibility of any citizen. The first requisite of a good minister or good citizen is that he must be able and willing to pull his weigh. He must be able to walk-the-walk after he has talked-the-talk. Besides work within the church, Reverend Flanigan was very active in many different organizations whose primary missions were designed to promote and advance the lives of people from various backgrounds. It is an understatement that Reverend Flanigan has left his mark on the world in the shape of ideas, and in the form of good deeds. He continues to do so up to and including this very day.

After reading the manuscript, R. Larry Fullwood, former healthcare director with the Department of Veterans Affairs wrote, "It is my personal evaluation that Reverend L. Flanigan is all of the following and more:

A Man of Vision
A Man on Fire for the Lord
A High Energy Person With a Serious Sense of
Dedication and Determination to Succeed
A Man With an Open Mind Who is Eager to Learn More
And More
A Man With a Keen Thirst for Education for Himself
And Others Around Him
A Man With Boundless Faith in God and God's Glory
An Enlightened Pathfinder
A Natural Leader and Teacher
A Sincere and Charismatic Person
A Man With Wisdom
A Man at Peace Within Himself
A God Centered Man in all of His Activities
A Man Who is Kind and Generous to a Fault (Selfless)"

During his career, Mr. Fullwood has made a significant contribution through his editorial and proofreading skills that have enhanced the readability and improved the quality of numerous manuscripts, contracts and other government and private sector documents.

A Special Calling. This section provides background information on the featured person in this book, the Reverend Lud Flanigan. The chapter begins with the recognition that Reverend Flanigan has attained and maintained through the grace of God a superb memory. The chapter also provides a discussion of his birth, family life, ministry and church involvements and the active role he played in the community and in DeSoto Parish Public School activities.

Questions, Responses and Getting to Know Reverend Lud Flanigan. Several face-to-face meetings were held with Reverend Flanigan over a period of six months. During these discussions, a number of questions relating to his personal life were asked. The questions and responses thereto are presented in this section. Getting to know the Reverend Lud Flanigan is a charm! By anyone's measure, he is a kind, approachable, loving and not surprisingly, a down-to-earth gentleman. He has also had a better than average number of achievements in life. However, what we call achievements, Reverend Flanigan calls beginnings. His entire life history shows that he has been proactive and taken actions rather than sitting back and waiting to see what would happen. He always took it upon himself to get acquainted with key political officials in the city and in the parish as well. This required that he would have to establish meaningful ongoing contacts with principals, teachers and others who supported the DeSoto Parish School System.

I Remember Reverend Lud Flanigan. One thing is certain, during his ninety years plus and counting on planet earth, Reverend Flanigan came in contact with a vast number of people from all walks of life. He has attained a long list of people whom he claims as his life-long friends and associates. A few of them have provided comments regarding their personal knowledge and experience in working and/or worshiping with him.

Honors, Awards, and Recognitions. Reverend Flanigan attained numerous honors, awards, and recognitions during the more than 60 years of ministry and work within the community. However, just a few of those attributes he was able to retrieve are shown in this section.

The Bible. Each time the Reverend Flanigan appeared on the pulpit, he either had a Bible in his hand or had one placed on the podium directly in front of himself. It is safe to say that Reverend Flanigan spent most of his life reading and/or studying the Bible because his life's work is a living example of his enduring faith in God's Power and Glory and the principles of Faith, Hope and Love which are the corner stones of the foundation upon which his total existence depends. The Bible is the most read text in the entire world. On a daily basis, more people read the Bible than all of the other books combined. For these reasons, the Bible is discussed in this book in a separate section.

The Church and The Minister. The church is one of the oldest institutions in the world. Before his retirement, Reverend Flanigan served as pastor for twelve churches. This section describes how the local church is organized and operates. The minister's responsibilities within the local church go beyond providing a sermon on Sundays. His role within the church's mission is discussed in this section.

The Human Brain and Our Memories. The reader will find that the brain is the most complex thing in the universe and that it is also the primary key element in our memory process. Every part of the brain will be defined with regard to the role each plays in the function of the body.

The Force of Memory. Memory is a dominant force in life. All of us desire an excellent memory. An excellent memory sets the stage for success and exceptional achievements in all aspects of our lives. The reader will learn what studies and research have uncovered about the effect of memory. Memory Loss. Memory loss is a normal process and it occurs to all of us at one time or another. However, there are ways to preclude serious memory loss. Suggestions made by medical professionals and others are shown in this section. How Can One Improve Memory. Memory in humans can be improved in certain ways. Information in this section will disclose modern techniques one may use to enhance memory.

Longevity, Aging and Memory. The reader will get reacquainted with the word longevity which is the condition of living a long time. Aging will also be discussed as it has been defined as changes in an organism, organ, tissue, or cell leading to a decrease in functional capacity in humans. An overview of both longevity and aging will be presented with further focus placed upon modern human lifespan, advancements in medicine, technology and other evidences seen as why life expectances are increasing. The reader will also find that there have been considerable research and studies devoted to longevity and aging as they relate to the overall health and well being of individuals and memory.

The History of Mansfield, Louisiana. Mansfield, Louisiana is the birthplace of the Reverend Lud Flanigan. By any measure, it is most appropriate to trace how the city of Mansfield was discovered and progressed through the years to what it is today. The reader will learn that there are parishes in Louisiana opposed to counties as found in most states. Mansfield is located in DeSoto Parish as the state of Louisiana has a total of 64 parishes. As is found in most southern states, DeSoto Parish was occupied first by Native Americans. The chapter will provide an account of how DeSoto Parish and Mansfield, which is the parish's government seat, has grown and developed into a progressive small city.

History of DeSoto Parish Public School System for African-Americans. The establishment of a public school for African-Americans in DeSoto Parish is noteworthy. The education of children in a school setting began in the church in the 1600s. The church was the primary source of education until the 1800s. Public schools began to flourish in the mid to late 1800s. Public schools were made available to African-Americans in the early 1900s. The reader will find that public education for African-Americans obtained its roots in DeSoto Parish in 1913. It began with a two-room white frame building located in a piney-wood area in East Mansfield. The first principal of the school was DeWitt Johnson and his wife; Elizabeth was one of the first teachers.

Once the word spread that there was a public school for African-Americans within the surrounding areas, the enrollment immediately increased. The increase in enrollment caused a need for additional space and teachers. Over the ensuing years the physical plant and the number of teachers as well as the school curriculum were expanded. Other schools were built in the parish and they became successful as well prior to the closure of DeSoto High School in May 1979.

Achievements: Reflections of Greatness and Spotlights on Legacy. This section is a showcase of the individuals who excelled at DeSoto Parish Training School and/or DeSoto High School as instructors, coaches, and students. It recognizes the prowess of the football and basketball teams during the late 1950s and early 1960s. The showcase also includes those who have lead successful careers in a variety of professions after graduation from this exceptional school.

CONTENTS

Reverend Lud Flanigan

CHAPTER I

A Special Calling

The Reverend Lud Flanigan's life history is defined more for his superb memory than his preaching. However, most people have said that both are exceptional. More than the fourth child of a share-cropper; more than being a good citizen in a small southern city. Far more than a leader of the community in which he lives, including the entire state of Louisiana, the Reverend Flanigan has a special calling! He is an ordained minister, renowned community activist and possesses a superb memory at the young age of 90.

To test his memory abilities, one needs only to mention the name of a local citizen, former citizen, or anyone else he has met and Reverend Flanigan will take over from there. He will reveal where the person lived, the relatives by first names, where the person worked and what church the person attended. He knows and can recall most of his neighbors he has had over the past 65 years as well as the members of the churches where he was pastor, local political leaders, principals and teachers within DeSoto Parish and other ministers in the community. Mr. Nathaniel Lilly, former teacher and emergency preparedness director, who has known Reverend Flanigan since early childhood, in an interview for the preparation of this book stated that, "I will be meeting with Lud in the near future in order to find out more about some of my past relatives. He knows my family and he has proven to be a reliable historian and source of reference."

The Reverend Lud Flanigan was the fourth child of Wash and Liza Joyce Flanigan. Lud Flanigan was born on November 28, 1919 in a house on Oxford Road, located approximately five miles outside of Mansfield, Louisiana. His mother, like most wives in those days was a devoted housewife and stayed at home to prepare meals and raise the children. His father farmed

1

several acres of land as a sharecropper on the old Dave McCoy's and Jack Guy place. Lud grew up with his siblings, two brothers (Robert and Wash) and two sisters (Carrie Bell and Maggie) who were also born in the same house. Reverend Flanigan's father, Wash lived to be 88 years of age. However, he was a latecomer for publicly accepting Jesus Christ as his saviour. It was stated in a special dedication by the Paradise Baptist Church in memoriam of Wash Flanigan that his timing was not as important as the fact that when he arrived, the Lord welcomed him with opened arms. The dedication also stated, "Regardless of our age when we came to Christ, we all arrived late; and it was by His grace…not our works that we were saved at all. It matters not, moreover, which church claimed his membership, or who served as his pastor. For the church is the body of Christ, and Christ is the head of the church. He said, 'I have other sheep which are not of this fold.' We relate well to his conversion because in every human soul there is a saint and a sinner…a struggle between the forces of good and evil and because heaven rejoices over one sinner that repents, more than over 99 saints who need no repentance. Having been born in sin before we were born again, we all fall short of the glory of God. Wash Flanigan symbolized every man. His success is to be measured not so much by the status he held in life, as by the hardships and obstacles he endured and overcame before he died. On his death bed, the whole meaning of his life rested upon the certainty that Jesus Christ was his Lord and Saviour."

Reverend Flanigan's education attainment (prior to Coleman's College of Theology years later) includes completion of courses of study at Mount Olive Church Settlement School in Oxford, LA. During this time, all public schools' educational activities were held at churches and the highest grade of achievement was the seventh grade. Lud joined the Mt. Olive Quartet and traveled around singing at different black churches throughout the community. During his younger days, he played on the Jack Guy baseball team as a pitcher and said he dreamed of someday becoming a professional baseball player. He also attained further educational training at the DeSoto Parish Training School following the completion of study at Mt. Olive. Immediately following his course of study at DeSoto Parish Training School, he was asked and encouraged to attend Leland College, a private religious school located in Baker, LA, where he studied the Bible. The courses studied and completed at Leland College were taught under the umbrella of the state Bible Convention. The course of study was for the duration of approximately one year for which he received a graduation certificate after completion. He also received an honorary degree from Shreveport Bible College. He was called to preach in August 1940 under Reverend J.H. Fobbs and he stayed and served under Reverend Fobbs for four years.

On October 8, 1939, Reverend Flanigan married his sweetheart Dollie Short. They were happily married until she passed on to a greater place in 2003. They had three children, all boys; Louis, Wilbert, and Roosevelt.

Reverend Flanigan recalled that during the late 1930s and early 1940s, sharecropping was not paying enough money to support a family of three, so he went to work for Standard Oil Company. He prayed that God would show him the way to help his family and still be home to attend church on Sundays, and to be with his wife and son at night. Lud left Standard Oil and found a job as a laborer with a pipeline company in Lake Providence, LA until a leg accident caused him to leave after a year. He then went to New Iberia, LA working during the sugar cane harvest for several months. Since this job was not paying sufficient money to support his family, he went out to seek work and found a job as a truck driver with Charles Patterson Wholesale grocery Company in Mansfield.

Reverend Flanigan also recalled how he and his wife Dollie, owned and operated a dry cleaner business in Mansfield during the early 1950s for approximately two years. Mrs. Flanigan also performed various jobs within the community on a voluntary basis. She was very supportive and helpful in all of the churches in which her husband was pastor and refused to accept recognition for the services rendered.

All three sons were star football players at DeSoto High School in Mansfield, Louisiana. Wilbert and Roosevelt also lettered in basketball and baseball at the school. The trio also attended Grambling State University after graduation from DeSoto High School. Louis and Wilbert played football at Grambling State after receiving four-year scholarships in the sport. All three are married and are responsible for providing seven grandchildren.

Reverend Lud Flanigan was very active in the local community for many, many years. He is responsible for carrying the first group of African Americans to sing at the First Methodist Church on Polk Street in Mansfield. He was one of the first African-American to obtain a Social Security card in DeSoto Parish in 1937. Reverend Flanigan stated, "At that time a person had to be 21 years old before he or she could obtain a Social Security number and card." When the Polio (also known as Poliomyelitis) epidemic reached its heights in the early 1950s, Reverend Flanigan was asked to represent the DeSoto Parish's African- American community to attend a training conference in Tuskegee, Alabama to obtain information on the prevention and treatment of the disease. Polio was one of the most dreaded illnesses during this time and had killed or paralyzed thousands of people in the nation. As a direct result, President Franklin D. Roosevelt founded the March of Dimes as the National Foundation for Infantile Paralysis in 1938. Reverend Flanigan stated that it was believed back then that the President himself was paralyzed with polio. Reverend Flanigan's delegation was charged with obtaining pertinent information at the meeting in Tuskegee and shares it with local citizens upon their return to the community. He was among a group of five African-Americans who were the first of their race to register to vote in Mansfield and DeSoto Parish in the early 1950's. The other Four individuals in the group were Robert Jenkins, Burnet Boyd, Reverend Cleveland Tyler, and Walter Gardner.

He was also very supportive and active in DeSoto Parish School special events such as the Parents and Teachers Association (PTA). Reverend Flanigan was recognized for being instrumental in taking the lead role in assisting the President of the PTA in raising funds to acquire warm-up capes for the football team in the late 1950s. He was one of the leading citizens of the community to help obtain a separate building to house the school's band.

Reverend Flanigan was the first African-American to work as a disk jockey at the Mansfield radio station KDXI located on Delton Road. More than 55 years later, he described the exact location of the radio station on Delton Road as well as the best way to get there from both directions. His pay was based on a commission where he made announcements and advertisements for businesses that sponsored various programs at the station. While working there, an attempt was made to have him play blues, jazz and rock music as a form of entertainment. Even on September 16, 2009, he recalled reminding the radio station officials that he was a minister and refused to take on this assignment.

Reverend Flanigan's ministry spanned over a period more than 65 years, considering the time he spent serving under Reverend Fobbs. Between 1945 and 2004, he served as the pastor of twelve churches. The first church he served as pastor was in 1945 at the St. Joseph Baptist Church in Pelican, LA. He presided as pastor at St. Joseph Baptist for several years. The word spread that Reverend Flanigan knew the word of the Lord. Consequently, he was asked to serve as pastor at Gethsemane of Mansfield, St. Mark in Carmel, New Hope Baptist of Mansfield, Mose Chapel and St. Mark, both in Mansfield, Antioch of Pleasant Hill and Mt. Moriah in Kingston, LA, He also was pastor at Mt. Zion in Kingston, Mt. Calvery in Zwolle, and New Hope in Carmel. As demands increased for his services as minister, on many occasions he served as pastor of two or more churches at the same time. Following these experiences, Reverend Flanigan saw that he was in demand to lead the sheep to Christ, so he enrolled in Coleman's College of Theology to better learn how to lead his people. He studied at Coleman's College for several months before taking on his final church. The last church he served as pastor where he was the senior minister for more than 48 years was the Paradise Baptist Church, located in Shreveport, LA. While at Paradise his friends at Springhill Baptist Church persuaded him to come and pastor them. This he did, however; after several years he knew that Paradise needed him full time, as it was a rapidly growing church and he resigned as pastor at Springhill and devoted his full-time services to Paradise Baptist. On June 9, 1996, Paradise Baptist Church held its 77th anniversary. An excerpt from Reverend Flanigan's greetings were as follows: "Leadership is our legacy. It is our calling. It is our commitment and we shall continue to strain the muscles of our soul to ensure that this battle will continue to be won and that it will lead to victories that ultimately result in a greater sharing of God's good gifts and a greater roll call at Kingdom's door." On June 14, 2009, the church held its 90th anniversary. The church's anniversary program made the following statements in regard to Reverend Flanigan and his leadership:

"In August of 1955, the Lord sent Paradise an immovable and steadfast preacher by the name of Lud Flanigan, who became the pastor for an astonishing 48 years. Under the honorable Reverend Flanigan, the church made tremendous progress. On that faithful first Sunday in August of 1955, Reverend Lud Flanigan preached his first sermon as pastor of Paradise Baptist Church. Pastor Flanigan organized a host of deacons, deaconesses, church officers, trustees and many new members were added through Baptism, Letter and/or Christian Experience, who joined the forever growing congregation. While serving the Lord as pastor of Paradise Baptist Church, Reverend Flanigan organized eight active departments and saw a need for a much larger church facility.

This visionary organized a building committee, which consisted of deacons and members to research erecting a grander and much larger building to house the Paradise Baptist Church. The process was slow and the journey didn't come without struggles, but on May 1, 1966 at a total cost of $128,247.00, the building in which we currently hold services was completed. Fry Architectural and Engineering with the aid of C. K. Carter Construction, Co. presented the keys to the current edifice which stands at 137 feet, 8 inches long, 81 feet wide with over 8,000 sq. feet of floor space. The Church auditorium was built to seat 500 people; the choir stand was built to suffice a choir of 60 people. It also contained cathedral stained glass which lined the east and west sides of the church, as well as, the front of the church. Numerous classrooms, pantry, Baptistery, Pastor's Study, businesses offices and a mechanical room were all housed in the church.

Pastor Flanigan created a haven for those seeking the Lord. In 1996, for the church's 77th Anniversary, Pastor Flanigan wrote these words which still holds true today. 'When a church celebrates an anniversary, it's more than just a counting of years. It's age and longevity measured by purpose and service to God. Surely, in that regard the Paradise Baptist Church has strived to be a leader in saving souls for Christ and building up His Holy Kingdom. As it is so aptly articulated in the book of Joshua, the church can ill afford to be a follower or an institution, which seeks to maintain the status quo. By its very mission, the church has only one revered place in the eyes of God and that is a leader, teacher, builder, organizer, planner, endower and all of the other high places in the world order that signify leadership. The church must lead, and it must do so with GREAT passion and steady strides.'

The great preacher, minister, organizer and teacher retired January 4, 2004. He left a legacy of leadership and profound place in Paradise's history."

The church's anniversary program also made the following statements, which can be attributed to the exceptional contributions made by Reverend Flanigan and others in the church's success:

"Over the years since Paradise was founded, it has been led and directed by pastors, officers and a congregation which has sought to put God's word and his will first and foremost in their personal lives and in the lives of those in the community. Not every advancement or every task taken on by the church has been easily made; not every move forward has been readily accepted with open arms and willing hearts. However, God has seen fit that this church still stands readily available to those willing to seek his faith. The journey of 90 years has not been easy and the victories have not come without much struggle. The history of this church proudly proclaims that from the founding fathers to the present congregation there has been serious commitment to leadership.

The church is deeply indebted to those pioneers for blazing the way to such a strong Christian institution. Before our birth, the church gave our parents ideals of hope and strength that make our homes a place of love and faith. Our forefathers passed on to us this GREAT heritage through their faith in God and their faithfulness to the Christian task. With our increase in congregation, facilities and abilities we have a great challenge to extend the gospel to our children, in turn that they realize that faith is the substance of things hoped for and the evidence of things not seen. In hope that this church celebrates many more anniversaries, it must first continue to lead and must do so with great passion and steady strides."

During the period of his ministry, Reverend Flanigan delivered more than 2,100 sermons. These include sermons delivered at churches he served as pastor as well as at other churches and events where he had been invited as an evangelist. Twelve ministers have been called to preach under his pastorate. He married over 500 couples, and baptized well over 2,000 people during his ministry. He was invited to serve as the keynote speaker at many revival services throughout DeSoto, Caddo and surrounding parishes during the prime of his ministry. He was also invited to speak across the state line in Dallas and Houston, Texas on several occasions.

At its 29ᵗʰ Anniversary celebration, the Paradise Baptist Church saluted Reverend Lud Flanigan by making the following statements:

"As a preacher he follows the admonition of Jesus to Peter, 'feed my sheep.' We, at Paradise, have been recipients of this food, filled with ingredients of the Holy Spirit for believers, and with the essence essential to Salvation for the non-believer. Your continuity in the face of obstacles has been that attributed to Paul, 'for necessity is laid up me, yea, woe is me unto me, if I preach not the Gospel.' (I Cor. 9.16) For 29 years we have felt the impact of God's Holy Word as sermon after sermon you heralded the Gospel message as a 'voice crying in the wilderness,' and as being 'in the spirit on the Lord's day.'

As a pastor you accepted the role of an overseer and under-Shepard of God's flock of believers. You have followed the admonition of Jesus to his disciples, 'to teach them to observe all things whatsoever I have commanded you: and lo, I am with you always, even unto the end of the world.' In this teaching capacity our Pastor has let God's Word have top priority. He has never failed in instilling in us the right principles of citizenship, as he led us, and guided us in facing our civic responsibilities. Many of us, through his guidance, learned to appreciate the relation of Church and State as we were led to believe that only a good Christian can be a good citizen. Romans 13:4 tells us that 'he is good for us.'

Our friend has exemplified the spirit of the trinity, three in one, as he added friendship. His friendliness is a reference word in his character and character is what a man is judged by...For each member he has time to listen to a problem, and help where possible. He is eager to give friendly counsel to those who desire it. We at Paradise have learned that we can depend on Reverend Lud Flanigan to assume the role of a friend when the going gets rough. For these reasons, WE SALUTE YOU, PASTOR, PREACHER, FRIEND."

Reverend Flanigan has received numerous honors, awards, and recognitions for his leadership in the church as well as for his community involvements over the past 70 years. Some of the awards for outstanding services, appreciations and outstanding community leadership contributions, will be listed in Chapter IV under the heading, "Honors, Awards, and Recognitions."

CHAPTER II

Questions, Responses and Getting to Know The Reverend Lud Flanigan

Questions and Responses:

Reverend Flanigan and I met on several occasions to discuss information that was considered important for creation of the manuscript for this book. For our discussion on October 13, 2009, I had prepared a list of specific questions I wanted to ask him for the record about his personal life, immediate family, and other people he has met over the years. Without reservations, he responded to each question specifically.

Question: What is your current daily routine? Response: "I work in my garden on most days. I like working in the garden. This has been my practice for many years. I enjoy doing the tilling of the soil, planting, fertilization as well as the harvesting of the vegetables. Working in the garden allows me an opportunity to get away from the regular routine of being in the house watching television or just doing nothing. I also get around within the community to lend myself as a helper to some of my neighbors and elderly people who cannot do things for themselves. I run errands for them and anything else that they may want me to do for them."

Question: What are some of your hobbies? Response: "Gardening, fishing and hunting are my hobbies. I have participated in these hobbies for many,

many years and still enjoy all of them. Your parents, grandmother and I were great fishing buddies when they were living. We used to fish together on Clear Lake as well as on Smith Port after it was built. On most days we would leave home early in the morning and return just before dark. We made it an all day affair and we knew where to find the big ones. I remember when the dam was built at Smith Port in order to form the lake. Before the dam there was no lake. Smith Port is a man-made lake and the water actually draws from Clear Lake. Before we owned boats, we would rent them from the owner at the lake store. I also still enjoy hunting in the fall and winter months. My son Ruth (Roosevelt), comes at least once a year to join me on my hunting trips."

Question: Did your brothers and sisters stay around Mansfield after they had grown up? Response: "They all stayed in and around Mansfield after they had stayed for a while to help out on the farm my father worked. My older brother worked at Standard Oil company in Shreveport but continued to live in Mansfield until he retired. My other brother and sisters all stayed in Mansfield and worked in various types of jobs in the city. They all were church-going people and kept to themselves over the years before they passed."

Question: What is your secret for a long life? Response: "The primary thing I do is keep busy, mostly helping other people. Another key factor is that I never worry a lot about things in life. If there is a problem, I take it to the Lord in prayer. I never take problems or challenging things to bed with me. I leave them outside or by the bedside, have a good night sleep and get up the next morning refreshed and deal with new things in a passionate and positive way. Another thing is that I stay away from gossip. To avoid gossip, I have learned that if I am in the garden working, most people will not stop to talk in the hot sun while I am working in it. They would say something like, 'hello reverend, I just passed by to see how you were doing. I won't disturb your garden work.' And most of them would keep going on someplace else. If there were business to discuss about the church affairs I would schedule a business meeting and discuss it at the church if possible."

Question: You stated that you never worry about things in life. Do you worry about anything at all? Response: "No. Why worry? Not worrying about anything I face in life is probably the primary reason I have lived as long as I have. God has no limitations on what we can go to Him in prayer for. I ask God to give me the ability to deal with things that can be changed and I leave the things I cannot deal with or change up to Him."

Question: I have a list of people who finished high school the same year (1962) that your son Roosevelt and I did. They all lived in or around East Mansfield neighborhood. Can you tell me what you know about any of (Freddie Henderson, Myrtle Rawls, Loree Jackson, Johnny Louise Fuller, and Rudolph Washington) them? Response: "I knew all of their parents. The Henderson fellow is now a minister and a high ranking official in the Methodist Church. The Rawls lady father's name was T. L. and she has a brother who now lives near Oxford Road in Mansfield. The Jackson lady who lived up the street from here got married after she finished school at Grambling College and moved to Texas. The Fuller lady lived just a few houses down this same street (Gibbs) was related to the Hewitt family who lived on the same street (Willard) you and your family lived. Rudolph Washington and his family used to live on Roach Street before all of them grew up and left. He also went to Grambling after finishing at DeSoto High School. His sister Christine now lives on Mary Street, not far from where the funeral home used to be. I know all of them because their parents were like brothers and sisters to me."

Question: What is the secret for your superb memory? Response: "I do not have a special secret on how or why I can remember things of the past. I do have a passion to know people I live around and those who I come in contact with everyday. Observing people that I come in contact with has always been a part of my life. I have learned a great deal by getting to know people in the city, churches and other places where I meet them. As I meet people in any setting, the contacts seem to remain in my memory without any type of efforts to store them there for future discussions."

Question: After retirement, do you miss any involvements with the church activities and/or members? Response: "Yes, especially my involvement working with the young children in seeing them growing up in the church. I always found a pleasure in seeing them developing into responsible Christian men and women in the community. Some of the children I saw shortly after they were born, I saw them in Sunday School and church services, I baptized them and then in many cases, I married them in the same church they attended."

Question: What are some of the changes that you have seen in the church? Response: "One of the things I have recognized that has changed is the way people dress for church. Women now wear pants to church as a common practice. In the 'older days' women did not wear trousers to church...they always dressed up with big hats on."

Question: What advice do you have for our young people today on having a successful life? Response: "I follow the message described in Proverbs 6:22 in advising young people on how to live. The verse states, 'Teach a child how he should live, and he will remember it all his life.' Young people must have a strong passion to achieve something in life. I feel that a person, especially young folks, should be compelled to do more than just enough to get by. I have always emphasized that a person's desire, not his or her IQ or parents' status within the community determines his/her destiny. The greater the person's desire, the greater his/her potential in life. Great passion or affection for life will increase a person's willpower to succeed beyond the average. I stress the fact that if a person wanted something badly enough, he or she would be willing to pay the price to achieve it. In the Bible, in the book of Revelation, chapter 3, it describes how God felt about a lukewarm attitude. An indecisive person will not get far with God. This is also described in the Bible in James 1:8. Deep passion will change a person as he/she grows up in life. When a person desires are in harmony with God's will, and that person follows them with passion, he/she cannot help but become a more meaningful and productive person. Young people today must remember a committed passion of doing the right thing will make an impossible thing, possible. Sometimes young people are influenced by shortsighted remarks made by their friends or peers and even by so-called experts: In 1798 Robert Fulton was made fun of and was told he would never invent a steam-driven boat that would be used to transport people and other things over water. Orville and Wilbur Wright were criticized at first in their efforts to build a heavier-than-air flying machine. Most computer experts did not think it was possible when William (Bill) Gates pioneered the first computer software on April 4, 1975. All of us should always remember that with God all things are possible as highlighted in Mark 10:27. When we become and continue to be passionate about God's purposes, He will show us the way and what is possible. I instilled this determination of passion within my three sons as they grew up and until they left to be on their own in life."

Question: What can you tell the readers of this book about your three sons? Response: "I can tell them that all three were brought up being taught and shown how to live the qualities of duty, integrity, passion and honor toward others. They learned from me, their father, at an early age that they had to work for what they would attain in life. When they were growing up in this house they were encouraged to help our neighbors and particularly the elderly by doing certain things for them that they could not do for themselves. They were encouraged to mow some of the neighbors' yards during the summer as well as perform other duties a young man could handle. They were not expected to get paid for these duties. This practice has been carried over into their adult life. This approach would also foster a good leadership charter for them. All three became quarterbacks on their high school football teams. They were encouraged to continue their education that would enable them to be even more supportive of others who needed assistance in life. Most importantly, they were taught to recognize that God had to be in the center of the equation of everything in their lives."

Getting to Know The Reverend Lud Flanigan:

"The World", Shakespeare wrote, "is a stage; sometimes events are staged in that world on a scale and with consequences that boggle the mind."

On the surface, Reverend Flanigan appears to be a kind, approachable, loving and down-to-earth person. But as the saying goes, he may look like a kind person, he may talk and act like a kind person; however, do not let anyone mislead you. He is indeed a kind hearted, approachable, loving, down-to-earth, caring person. Each time we met to discuss development of the manuscript, he was more than being a friendly person. In talking with him and the people who know him I found out that he was the kind of person everybody wanted to know and interact with. He always gave people he met a sense of confidence even before he observed that the person had some feeling of insecurity. He felt and expressed the reality that when nothing else works, God's word does. He knew that everybody he came in contact with had a need to feel special and he accommodated him or her by complimenting him or her in some way. He complimented people face-to-face as well as on occasions when he talked about them in their absence to other people. He certainly knows how to make people feel important. He gives everybody he meets hope. This is accomplished by letting people know that when they put God in the center of their lives, the future can be better than the past and present. A quote from the Bible supports this belief: "As long as he sought the Lord, God made him prosper" (II Chronicles 26:5). He has a characteristic that is not common for most ministers. He listens to what people have to say because he feels they need to be understood. He asked, "How can one help another person if he does not understand the problem?" This approach may take more time in dealing with an issue but it has shown to be most effective in the resolution of most people's problems. There is no need to be in a hurry to hand out advice and move on to something else. In this complex and often confusing world, he said, people need role models. Reverend Flanigan knows this phenomenon and he is indeed a role model for young and older people.

He is very much aware of the example he sets and the overall impression he is making every time he gets up in the morning. He stated that, "Like it or not, what we do and don't do influences others. When we leave this world, what we leave behind is our influence."

It was mentioned in an earlier section of this book that Reverend Flanigan played baseball during his younger years. Undoubtedly, baseball was by far his favorite sport and pastime. His favorite professional baseball team was the Dodgers and he followed them vividly before the team moved from Brooklyn, New York to Los Angeles, California. He had special regards for Jackie Robinson and knew him when Jackie played for the Montreal Royals of the Class AAA International League. Jackie Robinson joined the Brooklyn Dodgers on April 11, 1947, breaking the color barrier in major league baseball. Reverend Flanigan remembers that it was an exhibition game between the Brooklyn Dodgers and the New York Yankees in 1947 where Jackie played and this was the first time an African-American baseball player had been a member of a major league team. He spent many evenings listening to the Dodgers' games on the radio back in those days long before the event of television.

It was recognized in the initial chapter of this book that Reverend Flanigan grew up in the church. He attended Leland and Coleman Colleges where he studied the Bible. He also was a pastor of twelve churches over a period for more than 65 years. Consequently, it can be said without reservations that he has been reading the Bible his entire life. It is not surprising to learn that Reverend Flanigan embraces the contentions about the Bible as described by Bill Wiese in his book entitled, "23 Minutes in Hell." Mr. Wiese gave reasons why we should believe the Bible. He wrote, "The Bible is not just 'a' book, but a collection of sixty-six books written by at least forty authors over approximately a fifteen-hundred-year period. The authors were historians, military generals, prophets, kings, politicians, a doctor, a rabbi, fishermen, and even a tax collector. It was written on three continents and in three different languages: Hebrew, Greek, and Aramaic. They all wrote about the coming Savior. Every word was inspired by God. The famous poet Voltaire said that within one hundred years of his time, Christianity would be 'swept from existence and passed into history.' Yet fifty years after his death, the Geneva Bible Society used his house and printing press to produce stacks of Bibles. Jesus Himself made this statement: 'My words will by no means pass away' (Mark 13:31). Dr. H.L. Hastings a well-known writer, is cited saying, 'If this book had not been the book of God, men would have destroyed it long ago. Emperors and popes, kings and priests, princes and rulers have all tried their hand at it; they die and the book still lives.

There are more than three hundred prophecies in the Old Testament in regard to the birth, life, death, and resurrection of Jesus. No other book has been written foretelling the future with such accuracy. Professor Wilber Smith, DD, who taught at Fuller Theological Seminary and Trinity Evangelical Divinity School, said, 'Not in the entire gamut of Greek and Latin literature… can we find any real specific prophecy of a Savior to arise in the human race…neither can the founders of any cult in this country rightly identify any ancient text specifically foretelling their future.' The Bible 'is the only volume ever produced by man, or a group of men, in which is to be found a large body of prophecies relating to individual nations, to Israel, to all the people of the earth, to certain cities, and to the coming of One who was to be the Messiah.'

Many books have been written by some of the most competent scholars and well-educated individuals proving the validity of the Bible."

Reverend Flanigan has had more than an average number of achievements in life. Since achievement has been discussed a lot over the past several years, perhaps it should be defined. Achievement according to most dictionaries, is the result of effort or toil when successful; feat; deed; accomplishment; being able to look back and see how far you have come. Ralph Waldo Emerson wrote back in 1844 that, "The reward of a thing well done is to have done it." Even further back than that in 1737, Benjamin Franklin said, "Well done is better than well said." Achievement is one of the things that separates man from other animals. It is one of the things that we recognize just about every month in today's world. We have Halls of Fame, Emmys, Oscars, Nobel and Pulitzer Prizes and thousands of other formal types of recognitions of outstanding achievement. If for some reason a ceremony was not held to show recognition for any of these achievements, a number of people would protest why it was not done. Who's Who in America grows larger with every edition. The number of new products available and the new inventions, which make life easier from generation to generation, all testify to mankind's thirst for more achievement.

What most of us call achievements, Reverend Flanigan calls beginnings. Reflecting upon this, he can vividly relate to a statement made by President Dwight D. Eisenhower on April 2, 1957, when he said, "We succeed only as we identify in life, or in war, or in anything else, a single overriding objective, and make all other considerations bend to that one objective." This single overriding objective in Reverend Flanigan's life was serving and delivering God's word. A number of gratifying collaterals have emerged from this practice. At the young age of 90, it is clearly obvious that longevity has been achieved although a great life span was never his goal. God has blessed Reverend Flanigan with a unique talent…a superb memory. He can recall events and conversations that occurred ten years ago. However, what is most astonishing about his memory is the fact that he can clearly recall in detail, events, conversations and the people involved that occurred 20, 30, 40, 50, and even 60 years ago as though they occurred yesterday.

Reverend Flanigan can easily recall the major developments that have occurred in the history of the city of Mansfield and DeSoto Parish. As presented in an earlier section, most of the major developments occurred after his birth in 1919. He had an opportunity to meet and work with all of the political leaders from both the city of Mansfield and DeSoto Parish. In addition to his representation of the African-American community regarding the fight against polio through taking anti-polio vaccine as previously mentioned, he was also called upon to take the lead role pertaining to other community-related projects in the African-American community such as the installation of fire-hydrants, streetlights, water and sewer lines, and sidewalks leading to schools.

He knew all of the principals, teachers, bus drivers, and custodians who worked at DeSoto Parish Training School, DeSoto High School and DeSoto Junior High School. Reverend Flanigan knew Principal L.G. Jacobs personally as he remembers that Mr. Jacobs was born in Grand Cane, LA and that they played baseball against each other during their younger days. He also knew where all of the new teachers came from prior to their employment at the school. In our discussions we had about the difference teachers, he told me exactly where each new teacher lived when they first came to work at the school. As example, he mentioned that Mrs. Norvella G. Whitaker (known at the time as Miss Goree when she came to Mansfield) lived in the second floor apartment behind the R.D. Roundtree's Grocery Store. Since there were not an abundance of apartments in Mansfield for African-Americans at the time, many of the new female teachers stayed with established families and paid rent to do so. He recalled observing that coach Willie Robinson lived by himself in a small house across the street from the school. He thought coach Robinson lived in this house for many years until he eventually retired from the school.

Reverend Flanigan enjoyed an on-going dialogue with most of the teachers throughout the year, especially with head football and basketball coach C.D. Baldwin and his assistant coaches Willie Robinson, Clyde Washington, and James Jones. When Mrs. Norvella Goree Whitaker arrived in Mansfield in 1954, it did not take long for them to get acquainted and this friendship has been maintained to this day.

Throughout his adult life, even before his eldest son, Louis started school, Reverend Flanigan established and maintained an active role and participation on the Parent-Teacher Association (P.T.A.). He worked closely with every president of the association in bridging any possible gap that might existed between the teachers (including the principal) and parents. He often sought how the association could make the teachers' efforts less burdensome.

Getting to know different people throughout the community came natural for Reverend Flanigan. He has a God-Given talent of remembering just about everybody he meets. Not only does he remember their names and where they live, but also recalls certain personal histories pertaining to these same people. In one of our conversations, he mentioned that one of my sisters, "the one that married the Glenn fellow and lived near the old St. John Baptist Church," was among the first African-Americans to work at the DeSoto Parish Medical Center after it had been built in the early 1950s. "And she worked there for more than 30 years. There was another sister of yours (Rosie Harrison) who also worked at the hospital for many years before she retired. Now, she lives on this same street (Gibbs)." I asked my sister, Leola Glenn, was she one of the first Blacks to be hired at the medical center and she said, yes. She recalled that another African-American lady had been hired there just before she attained employment at the hospital. My sisters related that they used to observe Reverend Flanigan visiting patients at the hospital even after he had gone to another church and the patients were not members of his current church at the time of his visit.

Reverend Flanigan mentioned that he was a member of the same so-called "fishing club" in which my mother, grandmother, great aunt, and Willie Copeland belonged to. The group, after they had first started going fishing together, had to rent boats in order to go out into the lake to fish. A few years later, most of them bought their own boats and did not have to worry about what time they arrived or left the lake area. There appeared to be some type of existence of competition among the members of the group. Once, after my mother had returned home after a fishing trip, I overheard her talking on the telephone. She asked the person on the other end, "How many did you catch?" Apparently, the person on the other end of the telephone gave her a number. Then, my mother said, "Well, I beat you today. I caught 36, but most of them were small white perch." From this overheard conversation, I learned why my mother never took our suggestion to throw the small fish back in the lake. My brothers, sisters and I used to encourage our mother to throw the small fish back in the lake and hoped that she may have an opportunity to catch them again after they had gotten larger. She would listen to us but she never accepted our suggestion and continued to bring the small ones home for us to clean for our dinner meal.

During one of the sessions in which I interviewed Reverend Flanigan, he made a statement that he never worried about things in life and asked the question, "Why worry?" This question reminded me of a poetic statement I read once that was written by an unknown author. Excepts from the writing were: "There are only two things to worry about; either you are well or you are sick. If you are well, then there is nothing to worry about; but if you are sick, there are two things to worry about; either you will get well or you will die. If you get well, there is nothing to worry about. If you die, there are only two things to worry about; either you will go to Haven or to hell. If you go to Heaven, there is nothing to worry about, but if you go to hell, you are in a lot of trouble."

CHAPTER III

I Remember Reverend Lud Flanigan

Nathaniel Lilly, Teacher, Adult Education Instructor, Emergency Preparedness Director:

Mr. Lilly was reared by his mother and grandparents. He never saw his father until he was 56 years old. He attended elementary school in Trenton, LA in a one-room schoolhouse with 90 pupils, grades 1-5. The school sessions were gradually increased from 3 months to 8 months.

He graduated from DeSoto Parish Training School in 1947 after serving a tour in the US. Air Force. After a tour in the Air Force, Mr. Lilly was able to attend college for 27 months under the GI Bill that had been enacted by Congress for veterans to continue their education at the college level. He stretched the 27 months eligibility to 4 years by cutting off his GI Bill entitlement after he got his tuition and books paid for. He remembers following his math teacher to a college that was out in the country of Baker, LA named Leland College. The math professor was kind enough to give him a job working in his office.

Mr. Lilly's education attainments include a B.S. degree in Science from Leland College, a B.S. degree in Education from Grambling State University, and a Master degree in Education from Southern University. He also did additional graduate work at Louisiana State University, in Shreveport and Baton Rouge, Northeast (now University of Louisiana at Monroe), Southwestern University at Lafayette, Northwestern University at Natchitoches, University of South Dakota at Vermillion, SD, Southwestern Oklahoma State University at Weatherford, OK, Bishop College at Marshall,

TX, Texas Southern University at Houston. He earned more than 30 hours of credits above the master degree level. He also attended three trade schools during his teaching career: Photography, Black & White Development; Electronics, National School at Los Angeles; and Insurance, writer for CUNA MUTAL Credit Union.

Mr. Lilly's pursuit of a formal education and his work experience are very much intriguing. He attended summer schools and night classes over half of his entire career. He completed his Bachelor degree in Science in 3 years and 2 summers with a pre-med course in addition to a certification in chemistry, biology, mathematics, and general science. His first certification was in high school material instruction. After working at DeSoto High School for 8 years in mathematics, he was assigned to Grand Cane Community School. At Grand Cane, he taught 7th and 8th grades and earned certification in elementary education. He completed certification for grades 1-8 in 1962. He later earned certification in Adult Education. Mr. Lilly worked in the DeSoto Parish School System for 40 years as a teacher plus an unknown number of years as an Adult Education Instructor at night. His last seven years in the school system was spent serving as Director, Adult Education Center. After retiring from the school system in 1989, Mr. Lilly was hired as the first African-American to serve as Assistant Director for Emergency Preparedness. After the Director died, he was appointed Director until the organization was reorganized. He joined the DeSoto Parish Alumni Association grandparent program where he currently does volunteer work helping elementary children.

I have some personal knowledge of Mr. Lilly. I grew up in Mansfield, LA and lived next door to Mr. Lilly's first cousin, Samuel Pegues. Samuel and I often visited Mr. Lilly during the summer. Mr. Lilly was always busy typing something on the typewriter when we went by to visit. One day he asked had we read a book recently. I said yes and he asked me to summarize what I had read. As I was describing what I had read, he typed the information on his typewriter. I was proud of myself that he had an interest in what I said and he took the time to put it in print. He later informed me that the story I told would be used in a project he was working on for continuing education.

No one knows the Reverend Flanigan better than Mr. Nathaniel Lilly. Mr. Lilly informed me that he has known Reverend Flanigan, "since I was less than 3 years old." Mr. Lilly provided the following account about his relationship with Reverend Lud Flanigan: "My grandfather selected an area to farm that was nearly in the middle of Frost Johnson Lumber Company track of land and timber. There was no International Paper Company, and this company did all the lumbering in this area. In some areas, the timber man had his own train in the forest.

I got to know Reverend Flanigan because his mother and my grandmother were the best of friends. They were such friends that when they got ready to leave from visiting each other home, one would go a piece of the way with the other and this act went backward and forward long enough for the farthest one from home could have been there long before they did arrive home.

Reverend Flanigan was about 8 years older than I was. During my family visitation, as I being the oldest boy, I would have to travel with my mother or grandmother through the woods to see Reverend Flanigan's family. Reverend Flanigan and his brother would be working, I supposed since they were very seldom there when I visited. It meant that I sat alone or played by myself for the half-day or longer when we were at his mother's house. There was a little cluster of houses; a little over a 100 yards from Reverend Flanigan mother's house. I knew some of the children there and I wanted to go over and visit with them, but my mother would not let me go.

As I grew older, I knew Reverend Flanigan to be an active youth in Baptist Training Youth, Sunday School and church. There were rumors that Reverend Crook Robbins was grooming him for the ministry.

Reverend Flanigan mother's could always get some fresh vegetables, meat, syrup or what ever she needed. We were poor, but didn't know it. We didn't have the money but my grandfather, Jack Pegues had a 2-acre garden year-around. He would feed the whole community. We would kill about 8 to 10 hogs each year and cure them in the smokehouse. Our family as well as the entire community had meat throughout the year. Sweet potatoes were grown like they were raised for the market. We would have 8 to 10 potatoes stacked in the field like pyramids. After rain came, people from the community would come over and get what we had left in the field.

Reverend Flanigan's family did not have to worry about their share of anything. We carried supplies to his mother's house and his mother could get more whenever she visited us or whenever there was a need.

There were two churches across the woods that may have been two miles apart. I lived in between the two churches and I could hear both at night during the services from our house. Reverend Flanigan's church was Mt. Olive Baptist and my church Pleasant Valley Methodist. There were genuine cooperation between the two churches.

Through the forest when I got big enough, a few boys and I would sling blade and clear the trail of high grass, briar and logs to protect the women's stockings and legs from being scratched up. This was for the attendance of revival services at night at Mt. Olive Baptist Church. I can remember when I was a small boy when Reverend Flanigan's grandmother and grandfather were members of my church. The grandfather was the custodian and he rang the bell every 2nd and 4th Sunday for people to come for church services. I was at revival when Reverend Flanigan's father confessed Christ. From that day on I used to enjoy his father's shouting in church and running out doors.

Our baseball team of Trenton played Mt. Olive's team regularly. I think Trenton probably won a few more games than Mt. Olive. We had a few players that were major league caliber. For example, George Ross, a catcher, could always get the best out of a pitcher. Charlie Hill, our third baseman, could hit the long distance ball for anyone. If you were a base-runner, he would let you get two steps from the base and throw you out. There were other members who could have made it in the major league but I cannot remember their names. I do know that they were great because I saw Willie Mays in his 'hey days' play in the Astros-Dome in Houston, having to take some 'flies on the hop or bounce that one of our teams' players would have 'shoe stringed' those balls.

Reverend Flanigan was a young pitcher and I do not remember too much about his performance. These games took place between 1936 through 1939, when I was 9 to 12 years old. After that time, World War II disrupted the teams' playing and Reverend Flanigan was the lead singer of the quartet. I loved to hear him sing the Christmas song, 'Whom Shall I Send You' as well as the song, 'Precious Lord.' After Reverend Flanigan started his ministry, his brother 'White' became the lead man of the quartet.

About 40 years ago, Reverend Flanigan gave the eulogies for one of the baseball players he played against. The summary of his message was that its not important how many games you won or lost but it is important, how well you played the game as well as the game of life.

Reverend Flanigan was a great supporter of DeSoto High School. He fought for the citizens of Mansfield to have a better life and he is still fighting. He had three sons who were great athletes in high school, completed college and went on to be successful men."

Phoebia J. Bennett, Pastor's Aide Leader:

Mrs. Phoebia J. Bennett is oldest of 15 children in her family. Her 14 siblings include seven girls and seven boys. She was born on April 24, 1940 in Waskom, Texas.

Mrs. Bennett's family moved to Shreveport, LA when she was seven years old. Initially, the family lived with her aunt Mollie Tillman and this is when she started attending the Paradise Baptist Church. The church was led at that time by the Reverend C.F. Robinson. Mrs. Bennett was baptized in the church when she was eight years old.

Mrs. Bennett has been an active member of the Paradise Baptist Church since her baptism in 1948. She provided the following comments regarding her attendance at the church and how she worked with Reverend Lud Flanigan: "Reverend Lud Flanigan came to Paradise Baptist Church when I was 15 years old. I can recall when he preached his first sermon at the church in August 1955. He came to Paradise Baptist Church acknowledging that the church did not have much in terms of resources, but this fact did not stop him from preaching the gospel.

I was an active member of the church throughout my high school years. However, after I started employment, including working on Sundays, I was not able to attend church on a regular basis. I got married at the age of 23 and started having a family of my own. After having children, I knew it was time for me to get back into attending church because I wanted to bring them up in a church environment. By this time, the Lord was truly blessing Paradise Baptist Church. The pastor and members worked together successfully and were able to build a new church and even paid for its construction earlier than originally planned.

What I liked most about Reverend Flanigan was that he did not believe in the church selling candy, raffling tickets or doing car washing to raise funds for the church. We were able to raise funds to build the church and have other church related activities without doing any of these things.

I had five children that were active in the youth department and in the male chorus. I worked along with them in the youth department and was appointed president of the senior choir and also served as president of the pastor aides. Reverend Flanigan appointed me to be in charge of the church's kitchen as well as the supplies needed in dealing with the kitchen.

Reverend Flanigan is a person who does not forget. He is a person who always wanted to help people. I will never forget the contributions he has made to Paradise Baptist Church. He would work in his garden raising greens, peas, tomatoes, and other vegetables to provide for members of Paradise Baptist. He would bring truck loads of fresh vegetables for members to take home for enjoyment. Often, we would load up the church van and drive to Mansfield to gather up food from his gardens. While we were there, sister Dollie Flanigan would cook and feed all of us. They followed this practice for many, many years while he was our minister.

Reverend Flanigan is well known and he seems to know everyone in Shreveport that he has come in contact with…he remembers everything and everybody! There have been times where he would ask me about the people in Shreveport. I would say, 'Reverend I wish I could remember things and people the way you do.'"

James W. Cummings, School Teacher, Coach, Deacon:

Mr. Cummings is currently a deacon in Paradise Baptist Church. He was born in Camden, Arkansas and taught school in the state for two years before moving to Louisiana. Mr. Cummings, his wife and son moved to Shreveport, LA in August 1966 where he taught school in Caddo Parish for 33 years. He was also the football coach at Bethune High and Southwood High schools in Shreveport while serving as a teacher in those schools.

Deacon Cummings stated that when he and his family arrived in Shreveport in 1966 the Paradise Baptist Church had just been built at its current location on Hollywood Avenue. His family visited several churches in the community before finally deciding to join Paradise Baptist. The entire family was pleased with the church, how it was organized and enjoyed the way Reverend Flanigan preached. He also expressed, "When we first attended Paradise Baptist Church in 1966 I was very much impressed with the way Reverend Flanigan delivered sermons. We noticed that the church seemed to be a very good house of worship for children because there were many children in the church.

Reverend Flanigan is responsible for my being a deacon in the church. He encouraged me to become a deacon and I have been one now over 20 years. He also asked me to serve on the finance committee and shortly there after I was appointed to serve as the church's treasurer. Paradise Baptist Church grew considerably both physically and spiritually and also expanded its outreach under the leadership of Reverend Flanigan. I enjoyed working with him as our pastor and I extend best wishes to him in his retirement years."

Norvella Goree Whitaker, School Teacher, Basketball Coach:

Mrs. Whitaker is featured in section, "Reflections of Greatness and Spotlights on Legacy." I had an opportunity to observe her as she coached the girls basketball teams at DeSoto Parish Training School and DeSoto High. I can attest to the fact that she is a "winner"…the record speaks for itself. I also had an opportunity to converse with her on several occasions as we developed the manuscript for this book. Without any doubts, she is one of the most gratuitous person one would want to meet. Whenever she says that she is going to do something for someone, the person can be assured that it will be done!

Mrs. Whitaker had an opportunity to meet and get to know Reverend Flanigan and his entire family several years ago. She has never forgotten the first time they met. Her expressions regarding Reverend Flanigan were described under a titled she labeled, "Reverend Lud Flanigan (The Griot): From My Vantage Point." I have decided to reflect the entire articulation she wrote as follows: "We, born of a woman, are flawed and live in an imperfect world. Eric Larrabee stated, "Man is a flawed creature." I met the Flanigans (Dollie, his elementary school sweetheart-wife) in September 1954. Their youngest son, Roosevelt, was in my 5th grade class at DeSoto Parish Training School (DPTS)/DeSoto High School (now defunct). The Flanigans (and many others) were good thrifty parents who supported the school. They wanted not just their boys, but also all students to have a well-rounded education.

DeSoto school's campus was unique. I really have to look into my crystal ball to describe this school. Alright, let's see…I see some words and people. Extended families, resolve, camaraderie, stand patter, gleaners, prayers, creativity, singing and tall pine trees. Thank goodness, I didn't see any nay-sayers. Let me check again. Oophs, there is something way back in the shadows. It's blurry and hard to see. You are not going to believe this! It is a large crowd walking cautiously on a ledge. There are farmers, caregivers, scientists, domestic engineers, medical and legal professionals, mayors, warriors, entrepreneurs and many more.

We did not have a telephone, gymnasium, lights on the football field (basketball and football games were played during the day) nor grass on most of the school ground. We had a small student body, two short concrete walkways, a limited basic curriculum, a few restrooms, limited tables and chairs in the library, a few homemade bleachers and tall pine trees. Strong parental involvement made it possible for DeSoto to compete and excel academically and athletically with other (LIALO) AAA schools in the state. Someone said, 'It's not the size of the dog that's in the fight, it's the fight that's in the dog.'

Prior to entering the ministry, Reverend Flanigan sang in a quintet with J. B. Brown, Henry Brown, Johnny "Boy" Johnson and Tommy Scott. He pastored several churches before going to Paradise Baptist Church in Shreveport, LA. He is pastor emeritus and his work is not yet finished. He grew up during the depression and is not a hand-to-mouth retiree. Take a look at the following incidents:

— Incident # 1:

There were several male members who had an urge to try their luck a few yards behind the church building. He went outside where they were engaged and did not reprimand nor quote scriptures. They, the engaged male members said, "He merely knelt and prayed, got up and went back into the church building." They did not go there anymore. This was like a pebble dropped in the water.

— Incident # 2:

Awestruck, I saw him baptize my 27 year old husband-to-be in 1954. He had been wounded in combat (both legs and the right foot were crushed) on a hill at night in Korea. He refused a pain pill offered by the paramedic because he wanted to be able to cry out. Only God Almighty, through a fellow Mansfield soldier, Solomon Jackson, responded and carried him down the hill to safety. Recuperation was painful and tedious. He was grateful to the Almighty, Solomon Jackson and Reverend Flanigan. Reverend Flanigan baptized him and delivered the oration at his Transition on December 4, 1982.

— Incident # 3:

The Flanigans are close to nature and believe that able-bodied people should work. The nest was empty, but 3 freezers, chickens, hogs, fruits and vegetables abound. He has truck patches on other people's property. He is an outdoorsman and the squirrels had better watch out! We laugh at him behind his back and call him Johnny Appleseed. He will plant seeds here, plant seeds over there and everywhere.

— Incident # 4:

The Flanigans were misunderstood by some during their ORDEAL. With God Almighty, they were able to go through the Eye of a Legal Storm. We need to remember selective amnesia is a boomerang. Never criticize a man until you've walked a mile in his moccasins. - an American Indian Proverb.

— Incident # 5:

Two daughters, Ruby Hamilton Carroll and Dorothy Fuller Thomas, were fixated listening to Reverend Flanigan answer some questions at the public library. They sat on the edge of the seat , hands under their chins and soaked in every word. Isaac Hamilton, Ruby's dad, was a WWI veteran and known for his kindness and wisdom. Earnest "Tet" Fuller, Dorothy's dad, was ordained as a deacon by Reverend Flanigan at Mt. Moriah Baptist Church in Kingston, LA. Both men adored him.

— Incident # 6:

The Flanigans owned a store, a cleaners and still have rent houses. He was one of the first Disk Jockeys at KDXI radio station on Highway 84 West during the early 1960s. Dollie, his best girl, flew out to sea in 2002. He is still standing after being buffed around. He is somewhat like a Spider Lily. You can mow your lawn and two or three days later, the Spider Lily is in full bloom. And so it was!"

Louis C. Wells, Sr., Retired Military Officer, Deacon, Church Music Director:

Louis C. Wells, Sr. is a native-born Louisianan from Shreveport. He graduated from Central Colored High School in the same city. Mr. Wells and his wife Bettie M. had seven children, five boys and two girls. All of their children have attained advanced degrees from some of the leading universities in the nation, such as the University of Texas and Houston University, as well as the West Point U.S. Military Academy. A grandson, is a U.S. Marine and was serving in Afghanistan at the time the manuscript for this book was being developed.

Mr. Wells' military career spanned over 31and a half years before his retirement as an Army band director. He served on the faculty at the Naval School of Music in Washington, D.C. and was the first African-American to serve as director and Commanding Officer of the unit. While serving as band director, he lead his unit in playing for then President Richard Nixon's visit to the state of New York in New York City.

He attended seven colleges and universities and accrued more than 160 credits of undergraduate and graduate courses of study to attain his exceptional credentials to teach in the classroom and direct a band on the field. He also taught the Junior ROTC at Fair Park High School prior to retirement from the school system in Caddo Parish.

Mr. Wells joined the Paradise Baptist Church in 1983. His wife, Bettie was already a member and had been one for many years. He became a deacon three years after joining the church. During the late 1980s Reverend Flanigan asked Mr. Wells to serve as director of the music department. After praying over the opportunity he decided to accept the position. Sometime later, Reverend Flanigan was most gratuitous to offer Mr. Wells a salary to serve as music director but he refused the remuneration for his services to the church. He is currently serving in this capacity and has received several certificates of appreciation for his exceptional performance as director of the music department.

Mr. Wells was very complimentary of Reverend Flanigan as an individual leader and in his ministry in the church. He stated that, "Reverend Flanigan was a very gratuitous and outstanding God anointed preacher of the gospel or as we say, 'a person of the word.' In listening to just one of his sermons, one could tell that he had 'a special calling' to deliver God's word. His vision and insight in the building of the spirituality of the church was certainly noteworthy. He brought not only the spiritual aspect of preaching each Sunday in his sermons but his delivery brought many souls to Christ. Reverend Flanigan was gratuitous in brining the products of his labor from his garden as gifts to members of the church. All kinds of vegetables were brought in and given to members of the church where in many instances these food items were desperately needed by certain families.

As our pastor, he would listen to comments and recommendations if they were in the best interest of the church and were in consistent with divine guidance of the Lord. There are no doubts that he was called by God to serve as a minister. Last but not least, I must express the fact that his wife, Dollie, was a strong partner to Reverend Flanigan in leading our church. Whenever a group of us would visit to pick up vegetables to take back home or just visit for other reasons, Mrs. Flanigan would take the time to prepare a big meal and feed all of us before we drove back to Shreveport. She also participated in church related activities in a grateful way. She was an exceptional good person to know and work with."

Myrtle Rawls Turner, Teacher and Loree Jackson Washington, Author:

Both Myrtle R. Turner and Loree J. Washington were my classmates at DeSoto High School. Myrtle and I were classmates from the eighth grade throughout high school and college. Loree and I were in the same homeroom from the second grade through our senior year at DeSoto High. The three of us also attended Grambling State University the same year.

Reverend Flanigan knew the parents of Myrtle and Loree exceptional well. He knew exactly where each of the families lived as well as how many brothers and sisters each had while they were growing up. He knew where the parents worked and the churches they belonged to and what positions they served within the churches.

As a classmate, I remember that both Myrtle and Loree were exceptional students. Both made the honor roll each semester throughout high school and there was no doubt that they would attend college after they had finished at that level. While at college, they continued to excel in the classrooms and not surprising, both finished at the top of the class on graduation. Myrtle and Loree remain friends as Myrtle now lives in Shreveport while Loree resides in DeSoto, Texas. Mrs. Turner and Mrs. Washington provided the following remarks regarding the Reverend Flanigan:

"Who is Your Neighbor?

One neighbor of Reverend Lud Flanigan was my high school classmate and good friend. She remembers lovingly, Reverend Flanigan as a very kind but firm person. She remembers the kindness that he had shown to her elderly parents. Reverend Flanigan helped them with events in their lives that they did not quite understand as well as provided transportation for her parents when they needed to go to the store or an appointment. Reverend Flanigan, as a community person at heart, gave advice and guidance to all of the children living near his home. Teaching his children and the neighborhoods' children respect, morals and a need for Christ in their lives was an everyday job. Some of the things he stressed were putting a title on the names of adults that you speak to, for example "Good Morning Mr. Jones" as well as to always say "May I, please" and "thank you." This was truly practiced every day by Reverend Flanigan as he desired to see all children become God fearing, productive, intelligent citizens.

It is all about the Community:

If I allow my mind to travel back to where many might refer to as the "good ole days," I would choose to focus on the community where I lived. I was privileged to be in the midst of the great "Hall of Famed" known by all as Reverend Lud Flanigan. Reverend Flanigan was not only an observer, but a true participant in the affairs of the community. He challenged us as children and maturing adults to fix our hearts and minds on what we planned to do with the wonderful life we had been blessed to live. He was firm in the fact that it takes a village to raise a child. He was that kind of neighbor who would ask how well we did on report card day and how many A's and B's had we earned. So very encouraging was he, not only to me but to my parents as well. They were entering their aging years and he would offer them a ride to the store or pick up my father while he was walking home from town.

I was fortunate to be classmates with one of his three sons. Reverend Flanigan was very encouraging to his sons who were wonderful athletes. He would often insist that I get to my lesson and do my chores on time in order to be ready for the game. Of course we would be the first to arrive and the first to claim bragging rights with the other students.

All these wonderful attributes that followed him through the years began many years ago. Today is yesterday, the only change is the number in the year. This man is a sturdy, stalwart, a solid foundation rooted and grounded in the word of Faith and the works he can do for others.

Mere words are not enough to describe this notable icon. A heart as good as gold, forever encouraging always inspiring you to not be idle in your thinking, but move forward with your dreams, dare to accomplish whatever you desire. I am so proud to have been his neighbor and part of this community, to be in the number as one of the many who can proudly raise her hand in respect to a priceless gem. My heart swells when I'm asked do you know Reverend Flanigan. My response is and will always be I am honored to know him. If you had time to listen to a wonderful story, mine would be of a flaming torch lighting the way in community affairs and to anyone in surrounding areas who can find their way into the light that will forever shine brightly in my heart.

Reverend Lud Flanigan's Broadcasting Career:

Reverend Lud Flanigan was the first African-American radio announcer in Mansfield, Louisiana. He had a Sunday afternoon spiritual program, which gave opportunities for singing groups, choirs, and soloists to exhibit their talent on the air. What I remembered most from this program was the theme song, "Did you stop to pray this morning?" Not only did this song minister to me as a young person, it ministered to the elderly as well. This song enabled me to visualize the possibilities and blessings that could come from prayer if practiced daily. The elderly was able to reflect upon the power of prayer and from their experiences, they could see how prayer had changed things and events in their lives for the better. Reverend Lud Flanigan had an outstanding outreach ministry through this radio program. This program became to listeners in the black community, what television is to its many viewers today.

One Favorite Hobby Used to Edify God:

On any given day during the growing season, you may see Reverend Flanigan wearing his overall pants and his wide straw hat as he prepares to work in his garden. He is in my opinion, a person who is using one of his favorite hobbies (gardening) to minister to the needs of his neighbors and friends. Several members of his former church speak fondly of how he would harvest his crops of fruits and vegetables (especially watermelons) load up his pick up truck and drive to the church parking lot. There in the parking lot he would share his harvest with anyone who desired without cost. By the end of the day there would not be one fruit or vegetable left in that pick up truck. This was one of the numerous ways he would show kindness toward his fellowman. Even though this was only one of Reverend Flanigan's acts of kindness, this great deed did not go unnoticed. His gardening was featured in the local newspaper, The Mansfield Enterprise. To paraphrase Reverend Flanigan's very modest response when asked how he grew such large fruits and vegetables, he replied quite quickly, 'I planted the seeds and God gave the increase!'"

Wilbur T. Purvis, II, Funeral Director, Justice of the Peace:

Wilbur T. Purvis, II is a native of Mansfield, Louisiana and is a graduate of DeSoto High School. He has been a Funeral Director within the Mansfield community for more than fifty years. Many of the local citizens know him as they have come in contact with him in conjunction with his funeral services business and other support organizations. Mr. Purvis is a close friend of the Reverend Flanigan and they have known each other for many years. I learned just to the publication of this book that Mr. Purvis had been re-elected to serve as Justice of the Peace for DeSoto Parish.

Mr. Purvis met Reverend Flanigan through the relationship Reverend Flanigan had with his grandfather, W.B. Purvis. Reverend Flanigan met W.B. Purvis primarily because both were ministers as well as the fact that W.B. Purvis became a Bishop within the Louisiana African-American Baptist Association. According to the history of the association, Bishop W.B. Purvis served at one time, as the Corresponding Secretary for the Northwest Association for the Baptist state organization. He (Bishop W.B. Purvis) was described as one of the organization's best young ministers and in terms of actual service was surpassed by none. Reverend Flanigan made reference to Wilbur's grandfather and the Baptist state Association in many of our conversations.

Mr. Wilbur Purvis provided the following comments regarding how he became to know Reverend Flanigan, "I met Pastor Flanigan when I was a teenager. He would occasionally visit my grandfather who was also a minister. They would visit with each other long periods of time engaging in long discussions about the Bible and church matters. My grandfather was a much older man than Pastor Flanigan and I perceived in later years that he wanted to glean as much knowledge as he could from the older man.

Pastor Flanigan is steeped with a deep knowledge of family histories of many of the families in DeSoto Parish. He is an asset to so many families with his compassionate desire to be helpful when needed."

Tonya G. Washington, Military Retiree, Contract Specialist, Granddaughter:

Tonya G. Washington is the daughter of Roosevelt Flanigan and is the eldest grandchild of the Reverend Lud Flanigan. Ms. Washington is a U.S. Army retiree and currently resides in Madison, Alabama. She works for the Department of Army as a Civilian Contract Specialist in support of the war fighter in Iraq and Afghanistan.

Ms. Washington has always enjoyed a close relationship with her grandfather. She was happy to provide the following comments regarding their relationship: "When I was growing up, I spent a lot of time with my grandfather and grandmother. My grandfather and I have always had a good strong relationship and after Madea (Grandmother) passed, it became stronger. He is a wise, honest, trustworthy and dependable man whom I respect and love dearly. I always look forward to spending time and communicating with him. I call him at least two to three times a week so we may have conversations about difference things. When I call and the telephone is busy for an extended period of time or he does not answer when I know he should be home, I will call the next door neighbor or my cousins that live three blocks away to check on him. What I enjoy most is his storytelling and he has good jokes also. I often tell my co-workers, friends and people I meet that I have an extraordinary 90 year old grandfather whose memory is amazing, he lives alone, cooks for himself and still drives. Their response is, 'you are truly blessed.' Yes, I am blessed!"

Roosevelt Flanigan, Youngest Son:

It is not difficult to remember a person who has had a great influence on your life. It is not difficult to remember a person who has provided invaluable advice when you certainly needed it as well as at times when you felt you did not need it. It is not difficult to remember a person who you admired and looked-up to all your life and learned later that he was a role model for others as well. By anyone's measure this is most gratifying. It goes without saying that you will never forget growing up in the same household with a person who has had an exceptional impact on your life imprints that holds true today. These characteristics are fixed in the memory of Roosevelt, the youngest son of the Reverend Lud Flanigan.

Roosevelt was pitted in a challenging position while growing up and especially following in the footsteps of his two older brothers Louis and Wilbert who both were All-State outstanding football players at DeSoto High School in the mid to late sixties. But Ruth (nick name), as most of us called him, learned early on as he begin to participate in various sports that he would earn his own way through life on his own merits. He earned a distinctive reputation of being a tough competitor in every sport in which he engaged in. Ruth and I were teammates on the elementary school's basketball team, junior high's basketball and football teams, and high school's basketball, football and baseball teams. Some how or another, we always won more games than we lost in all of these sports. Most significant is the fact that Ruth was recognized as one of the leaders on all of the above mentioned teams. After leaving Grambling State University, Roosevelt completed a successful career with General Motors Corporation (GMC) and is now enjoying his retirement years in Wichita Falls, Texas.

Roosevelt cherishes the fact that he has been able to spend invaluable time with his father. This close relationship continues even today as mentioned in an earlier section of this book, the two have made it a practice to go hunting each year at the beginning of the squirrel hunting season.

Wilbert Flanigan, School Teacher, Football Coach, Administrator:

Wilbert is the middle son of three by Dollie and Lud Flanigan. He grew up in Mansfield, Louisiana along with Roosevelt and Louis. Although his parents were well established in the Mansfield community, Wilbert learned how to be successful in the performance of many laborious type jobs. He will not hesitate to inform anyone that he worked in the cotton fields in the early fifties, shelved food items at grocery stores in the mid-fifties, mowed yards and performed various other blue-collar type jobs until he finished high school. He did all these things and still maintained a proper perspective on education and preparing himself for life as a whole.

Wilbert graduated near the top (7th overall) of his high school class in 1960 at DeSoto High School. This was accomplished during the same time he lettered in basketball and football at the school. He is still considered one of the most astute and honorable athlete to graduate from the school. This is evidenced by the fact that he actually completed his college course work within three years instead of the customary four years.

He earned All-State honors as a star football player in high school. He was a versatile player as Coach Baldwin utilized him at both quarterback and halfback positions. He excelled at both positions most noticeably during his sophomore and junior years. Very few people are aware of the fact that Wilbert scored the first touchdown in Louisiana Triple A State Championship history when he scored a touchdown against Capitol High of Baton Rouge to win the school's second straight title in 1957. At Grambling State (then Grambling College), he started as a Freshman on the football team under the legendary coach Eddie Robinson in 1960.

Wilbert attained an illustrated career after finishing college. He taught school in the Springhill, Louisiana School System for 37 years. During this period, he was also the head football coach for Springhill High School where he was selected as the Coach of The Year in both 1967 and 1968. An exceptional indication of the quality of his work as a coach and character as an individual are exemplified by his selection to the Springhill Hall of Fame in

2002, the year he retired from the school system. He continues his residence in Springhill after retirement.

Wilbert was asked to make comments regarding his father, the Reverend Lud Flanigan. He stated that he had an opportunity to read the statements others have made and the things that he would say would be a replica of what the others have already said in which he agrees. However, Wilbert wants the readers to know that his father always placed great emphases on attaining an education. "Our father always told us that education in the modern world was very important to success. Education was very important to him...it ranked high on his scale just as important as freedom and fair justice."

Louis Flanigan, Eldest Son, Teacher, Football Coach:

As the eldest sibling, Louis always set the pace for his two younger brothers. He demonstrated leadership capability skills as early as in his elementary school years. Louis became the starting quarterback on the high school football team as a sophomore. Through his leadership, DeSoto High School football team won championships at the state's highest classification, three A level, for three consecutive (1956-1958) years. Coach Clarence Baldwin recognized that Louis possessed multiple athletic abilities when he was a freshman. Consequently, he utilized him on defensive teams where he excelled as a team leader.

Louis earned a four-year football scholarship at Grambling State University after his playing days at DeSoto High School. Coach Eddie Robinson recognized Louis' athletic skills immediately and used him frequently as both quarterback and defensive back. After graduation from Grambling State, he became head football coach at Walnut Hill High School in Shreveport, LA where he also was a classroom teacher for several years.

Louis' work and expressions relating to his father are pronounced throughout this book. This is evidenced by the fact that he played a key role in the development in the first publication of the DeSoto Parish Training School/DeSoto High School's Program and Souvenir Booklet for the school's All-Class Reunion, which described the history of the school for the first time in 1994. He is also responsible for a vast majority of the information presented in tributes, appreciations, recognitions, and celebrations extended by various churches in which his father was pastor.

CHAPTER IV

Honors, Awards, and Recognitions

The Reverend Lud Flanigan received numerous honors, awards and recognitions for exceptional services he rendered within the local community, at churches he served as pastor, and from other organizations he came in contact with over the past 65 years. A list of just a few of some of the honors, awards, and recognitions he received are shown below:

DeSoto High School Alumni Association
DHSAA/MFD Chapter
Recognized for: The longest living Black Minister of DeSoto Parish having the greatest number of years of service as a pastor with 75 years as pastor (27 years in DeSoto Parish and 48 in Caddo). "In the winter season of his life at the age of 88, he is still farming, A Greote, Community helper, Civic Advocate and a spiritual fed Minister."
June 26, 2009

North DeSoto Community Male Chorus
Leadership Award, "For Faithful Service as a Forerunner for Justice.
I have fought a good fight...I have kept the faith." II Timothy 4:7.
February 15, 2007

Paradise Baptist Church
Appreciation For Dedicated Service
Leadership of 48 Years: "Esteem them very highly in Love for their work's safe." II Thessalonians 5:12-13. Reverend Robert C. Hudson, Pastor
November 28, 2004

Paradise Baptist Church Youth Department
"Train a child in the way he should go: and when he is old, he will not depart from it." Proverbs 22:6.
August 11, 2002

Paradise Baptist Church
45th Anniversary Congratulation
August 13, 2000

Paradise Baptist Church
44th Pastor Anniversary (1955-1999) (Reverend Lud Flanigan)
"This Paradise family shall remain grateful for your loyalty, wisdom, kindness. You are a giver of God's work."
August 28, 1999

Paradise Baptist Church
30 years of Dedicated Service 1955-1985
August 12, 1985

Paradise Baptist Church
J.S. Williams Funeral Home, Minister of the Month Award
Certificate of Recognition
March 17, 1984

Paradise Baptist Church
30 Years of Dedicated Service (1955-1985)
"For I am not ashamed of the gospel of Christ: for it is the power of God unto salvation to everyone that believeth: to the Jew first and also to the Greek."
September 21, 1985

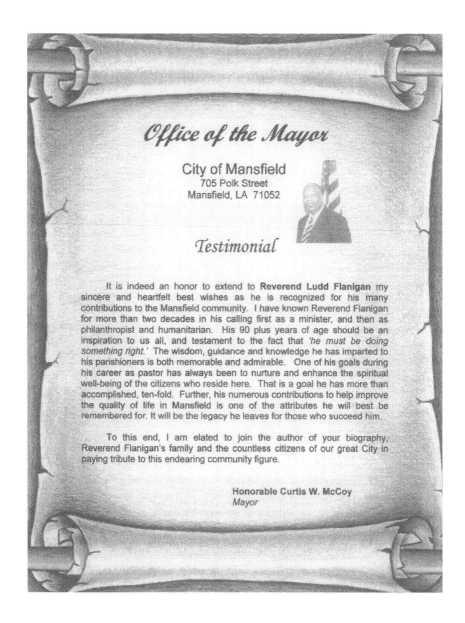

Office of the Mayor

City of Mansfield
705 Polk Street
Mansfield, LA 71052

Testimonial

It is indeed an honor to extend to **Reverend Ludd Flanigan** my sincere and heartfelt best wishes as he is recognized for his many contributions to the Mansfield community. I have known Reverend Flanigan for more than two decades in his calling first as a minister, and then as philanthropist and humanitarian. His 90 plus years of age should be an inspiration to us all, and testament to the fact that *'he must be doing something right.'* The wisdom, guidance and knowledge he has imparted to his parishioners is both memorable and admirable. One of his goals during his career as pastor has always been to nurture and enhance the spiritual well-being of the citizens who reside here. That is a goal he has more than accomplished, ten-fold. Further, his numerous contributions to help improve the quality of life in Mansfield is one of the attributes he will best be remembered for. It will be the legacy he leaves for those who succeed him.

To this end, I am elated to join the author of your biography, Reverend Flanigan's family and the countless citizens of our great City in paying tribute to this endearing community figure.

Honorable Curtis W. McCoy
Mayor

Chapter V

The Bible

The Bible, sometimes called the ***Holy Bible***, can refer to one of two closely related religious texts central to Judaism and Christianity--the Hebrew or Christian sacred Scriptures respectively. The term "bible" is sometimes used to refer to any central text of a religion, or a comprehensive guidebook on a particular subject. Judaism recognizes a single set of canonical books known as the ***Tanakh***, also called Hebrew Bible, traditionally divided into three parts: the ***Torah*** ("teaching" or "law"), the ***Nevi'im*** ("prophets"), and the ***ketuvim*** ("writings"). Canon is defined as sacred writings admitted to the catalog according to the rule. It is also referred to as the books of the Bible officially accepted by the church or religious body as divinely inspired. Canonical, taken from the word canon, means of according to, or ordered by church canon.

The Bible as used by Christians is divided into the Old Testament and the New Testament. The canonical composition of the Old Testament is in dispute between Christian groups: Protestants hold all of the books of the Hebrew Bible to be canonical and include them in what they call the Old Testament. Roman Catholics and Eastern Orthodox additionally consider the deuterocanonical books, a group of Jewish books, to be a canonical part of their Old Testament. The New Testament is comprised of the Gospels ("good news"), the Acts of the Apostles, the Epistles (letters), and the Book of Revelation.

The Tanakh (Hebrew) consists of 24 books. Tanakh is an acronym for the three parts of the Hebrew Bible: the Torah ("Teaching/Law" also known as the Pentateuch), Nevi'im ("Prophets"), and Ketuvim ("Writings," or Hagiographa), and is used commonly by Jews but unfamiliar to many English speakers and others (Alexander 1999, p. 17).

The Torah, or "Instruction," is also known as the "Five Books" of Moses, thus Chumash from Hebrew meaning "five some," and Pentateuch from Greek meaning "five scroll-cases." The Torah comprises the following five books: 1) Genesis, 2) Exodus, 3) Leviticus, 4) Numbers, and 5) Deuteronomy. The Torah focuses on three moments in the changing relationship between God and people. The eleven chapters of Genesis provide accounts of the creation (or ordering) of the world, and the history of God's early relationship with humanity. The remaining thirty-nine chapters of Genesis provide an account of God's covenant with the Hebrew patriarchs, Abraham, Isaac and Jacob (also called Israel), and Jacob's children (the "Children of Israel"), especially Joseph. It tells of how God commanded Abraham to leave his family and home in the city of Ur, eventually to settle in the land of Canaan, and how the Children of Israel later moved to Egypt. The remaining four books of the Torah tell the story of Moses, who lived hundreds of years after the patriarchs. His story coincides with the story of the liberation of the Children of Israel from slavery in Ancient Egypt, to the renewal of their covenant with God at Mount Sinai, and their wanderings in the desert until a new generation would be ready to enter the land of Canaan. The Torah ends with the death of Moses. The Torah contains the commandments, of God, revealed at Mount Sinai (although there is some debate amongst Jewish scholars as to whether this was written down completely in one moment, or if it was spread out during the 40 years in the wandering in the desert). These commandments provide the basis for Halakha (Jewish religious law). Tradition states that the number of these is equal to 613 Mitzvot or 613 commandments. There is some dispute as to how to divide these up (mainly between the Ramban and Rambam). It is divided into fifty-four portions, which are read on successive Sabbaths in Jewish liturgy, from the beginning of Genesis to the end of Deuteronomy. The cycle ends and recommences at the end of Sukkot, which is called Simchat Torah.

The Nevi'im, or "Prophets," tell the story of the rise of the Hebrew monarchy, its division into two kingdoms, and the prophets who, in God's name, warned the kings and the Children of Israel about the punishment of God. It ends with the conquest of the Kingdom of Israel by the Assyrians and the conquest of the Kingdom of Judah by the Babylonians, and the destruction of the Temple in Jerusalem. Portions of the prophetic books are read by Jews on the Sabbath (Shabbat). The Book of Jonah is read on Yom Kippur.

The ketuvim, or "Writings" or "Scriptures," may have been written during or after the Babylonian Exile. According to Rabbinic tradition and superscriptions to the Psalms themselves, many of the psalms in the book of Psalms are attributed to David; King Solomon is believed to have written Song of Songs in his youth, Proverbs at the prime of his life, and Ecclesiastes at old age; and the prophet Jeremiah is thought to have written Lamentations. The Book of Ruth is the only biblical book that centers entirely on a non-Jew. The book of Ruth tells the story of a non-Jew (specifically, a Moabite) who married a Jew and, upon his death, followed in the ways of the Jews; according to the Bible, she was the great-grandmother of King David. Five of the books, called "The Five Scrolls" (Megilot), are read on Jewish holidays: Song of Songs on Passover; the Book of Ruth on Shavuot; Lamentations on the Ninth of Av; Ecclesiastes on Sukkot; and the Book of Esther on Purim. Collectively, the Ketuvim contain lyrical poetry, philosophical reflections on life, and the stories of the prophets and other Jewish leaders during the Babylonian exile. It ends with the Persian decree allowing Jews to return to Jerusalem to rebuild the Temple.

The Christian Bible consists of the Hebrew scriptures, which have been called the Old Testament, and some later writings known as the New Testament. "Testament" is a translation of the Greek (diatheses), also often translated "covenant." It is a legal term denoting a formal and legally binding declaration of benefits to be given by one party to another (e.g., "last will and testament" in secular use). Here it does not connote mutuality; rather, it is a unilateral covenant offered by God to individuals.

The Old Testament consists of a collection of works composed at various times from the twelfth to the second century B.C. It was written in classical Hebrew, except some brief portions (Ezra 4:8-6:18 and 7:12-26, Jeremiah 10:11, Daniel 2:4-7:28), which are in the Aramaic language, a sister, language that became the **lingua franca** of the Semitic world. Much of it, such as genealogies, poems and stories, are thought to have been handed down by word of mouth for many generations. Very few manuscripts are said to have survived the destruction of Jerusalem in A.D. 70. The Old Testament is accepted by Christians as scripture. Broadly speaking, it is the same as the Hebrew Bible. However, the order of the books is not entirely the same as that found in Hebrew manuscripts and in the ancient versions, and varies from Judaism in interpretation and emphasis (see for example Isaiah 7:14). Several Christian denominations also incorporate additional books into their canons of the Old Testament. A few groups consider particular translations to be divinely inspired, notably the Greek Septuagint, the Aramaic Peshitta, and the English King James Version.

The New Testament relates the life and teachings of Jesus through the Gospels, the letters of the Apostle Paul and other disciples to the early church and the Book of Revelation. The New Testament writers assumed the inspiration of the Old Testament as formally stated in 2 Timothy 3:16: "Every God-inspired scripture is profitable to teaching...,"consistent with what New Testament scholar Frank Stagg says is the emphasis of the entire Bible on God' initiative in self-revelation and redemption. Stagg adds that the purpose of scriptures is served only when they bring one under the judgment and correction of God, leading to righteousness. The New Testament is a collection of 27 books, of 4 different genres of Christian literature (Gospels, one account of the Acts of the Apostles, Epistles, Epistles and an Apocalypse). Jesus is its central figure. Nearly all Christians recognize the New Testament as canonical scripture.

The Bible has always been central to the life of the Christian church. Bible scholar N.T. Wright says Jesus himself was profoundly shaped by the scriptures--the ancient Hebrew and Aramaic texts whose stories, songs, prophecy and wisdom permeated the Jewish world of his day. He adds that the earliest Christians also searched those same scriptures in their effort to understand what their living God had accomplished through the brief earthly life of Jesus. They regarded the ancient Israelites' scriptures as having reached a climactic fulfillment in Jesus himself, generating the "new covenant" prophesied by Jeremiah.

Chapter VI

The Church and The Minister

The Church:

Most people have heard of the word "church" and most think they know what a church is and what it does. The local church is a Christian religious organization made up of a congregation, its members and clergy. They are organized more or less formally, with constitutions and by-laws, maintain offices, sometimes seek non-profit corporate status in the United States and often have state regional structures. Church bodies often belong to a broader tradition within the Christian religion, sharing in a broad sense a history, culture and doctrinal heritage with other church bodies of the same tradition.

A local church may be an independently run congregational church and may be associated with other similar congregations in a denomination or convention, as are the churches of the Southern Baptist Convention or like German or Swiss Landeskirchen. It may be united with other congregations under the oversight of a council of pastors as are Presbyterian churches. Finally, the local church may function as the lowest subdivision in a large, global hierarchy under the leadership of one priest, such as the Pope of the Roman Catholic Church. Such association or unity is a church's ecclesiastical polity.

Among congregational churches, since each local church is autonomous, there are no formal lines of responsibility to organizational levels of higher authority. Deacons of each church are elected by the congregation. In some Baptist congregations, for example, deacons function much like a board of directors or executive committee authorized to make important decisions, although these congregations typically retain the right to vote on major decisions such as purchasing or selling property, large spending and the hiring or firing of pastors and other paid ministers. In many such local churches, the role of deacons includes pastoral and nurturing responsibilities. Typically, congregational churches have informal worship styles, less structured services, and may tend toward modern music and celebrations.

Local churches united with others under the oversight of a bishop are normally called "parishes." Each parish usually has one active parish church, though seldom and historically more than one. The parish church has always been fundamental to the life of every parish community, especially in rural areas. Most parishes have churches that date back to the Middle Ages. Thus, such local churches tend to favor traditional, formal worship styles, liturgy, and classical music styles, although modern trends are common as well.

Local parishes of the Roman Catholic Church, like Episcopal parishes, favor formal worship styles, and still more traditional structure in services. The importance of formal office is also a distinctive trait; thus a solemn mass may include the presence of officers of the Knights of Columbus as an escort for the regional bishop when he is present. Likewise, vestments are valued to inculcate the solemnity of the Holy Eucharist and are typically more elaborate than in other churches.

The Minister:

In Christian churches, a minister is someone who is authorized by a church or religious organization to perform clergy functions such as teaching of beliefs; performing services such as weddings, baptisms or funerals; or otherwise providing spiritual guidance to the community. The English word ***clergy*** derives from the same root as clerk and can be traced to the Latin ***clericus***, which derives from the Greek word ***kleros*** meaning a "lot" or "portion" or "office." Though Christian in origin, the term can be applied by analogy to functions in other religious traditions. For example, a rabbi can be referred to as being a clergy member.

A minister may serve a congregation or participate in a role in a Para church ministry. A person ministering to a particular congregation or religious group may be designated as a pastor. Ministers in other roles may be referred to as preaches, chaplains, deacons, elders, or bishops. An increasing number of charismatic Christians recognize the officers of the five-fold ministry, which they consider a revival of original Christian practice.

In Protestant churches, the word "minister" generally refers to a member of the ordained clergy who leads a congregation as its pastor. A minister may also participate in a leadership role in a Para church or allied ministry such as a street ministry, reaching out to those in the community who do not attend or regularly participate in church services or activities. Such a person may also be referred to as a preacher, chaplain or elder. A minister may also be designated as a bishop, but this is usually a hierarchical designation, for management or coordination of the church organization. A Chaplain as in English and/ or Almoner or their equivalents refer to a Minster who has another type of pastoral 'target group' than a territorial parish congregation, such as a military unit, school population, patients, etc. The Spanish Padre ('father') is informally used to address them, also in English. Elders in Christianity are involved in the collective leadership of a local church or of a denomination. A prelate is a member of the clergy having a special canonical jurisdiction over a territory or a group of people. Usually, a prelate is a bishop and sometimes refers to the clergy of a state church. "Father" is a term of address for priests in some churches, especially the Roman Catholic, Orthodox and Anglican traditions. In Christianity, an archbishop is an elevated bishop, responsible for all churches belonging to a religious group of a particular district.

In the majority of churches ordained ministers are addressed as The Reverend. However, as above, some are addressed as Pastor and others do not use any specific style or form of address, in which case it would be Mr., Ms., Miss or Mrs. as the case may be. In the Roman Catholic Church the form of address depends on the office the person holds, and the country in which he is being addressed as they are usually identical to the titles used by their feudal or governmental equals. In most English-speaking countries the forms of address are: A priest is usually referred to as Father; sometimes he is addressed as Your Reverence or Reverend Father. A bishop is addressed as Your Excellency or, less formally, Excellency. An archbishop is also addressed as Your Excellency or, less formally, Excellency. A cardinal is addressed as Your Eminence. The Pope of the Roman Catholic Church can be addressed as Holy Father or Your Holiness.

Depending on the denomination the requirements for ministry vary. All denominations require that the minister has a sense of 'calling.' In regards to training, denominations vary in their requirements, from those that emphasize natural gifts to those that also require advanced tertiary education qualifications for example from a seminary, theological college or university. There are several references in the Bible relating to leadership roles of ministers in the church and as a whole. One of the clearest references is found in 1 Timothy 3:1-16, which outlines the requirements of a minister or bishop.

The Roman Catholic, Orthodox, United Methodist (USA), Anglican and some Lutheran churches have three orders of ordained clergy: 1) Bishops are the primary clergy, administering all sacraments and governing the church, 2) Priests administer the sacraments and lead local congregations; they cannot ordain other clergy, however, nor consecrate buildings, and 3) Deacons play a non-sacramental and assisting role in the liturgy. Term rector (from the Latin word for ruler) or vicar may be used for priests in certain settings, especially in the Roman Catholic, Anglican and Episcopal traditions. A parish, which is responsible for its own finances is overseen by a rector. A bishop is nominally in control of a financially-assisted parish but delegates authority to a vicar.

The term Pastor tends to be used in many Protestant churches. Pastor comes from the Greek word ***poimen*** meaning shepherd and is a reference to Jesus' use of the title the ***Good Shepherd*** for himself. A person serving as a pastor will be assigned to a local church or congregation who may be referred to as his or her ***flock***.

In the ministry, as is in all other areas of work, there are certain issues that may permeate discussions among people from time to time. As example, there are contrasting views on the level of compensation given to ministers relative to the religious community. There is often an expectation that they and their families will shun ostentation. However, there are situations where they are well rewarded for success, whether measured through drawing people to their religious community or enhancing the status or power of the community. Having women as ministers is another issue. The acceptance of women in ministry has increasingly become an established practice within many global religious faith groups, with some women now holding the most senior positions in these organizational hierarchies. There continues to remain disagreement between the more traditionally fundamental global church denominations and within their denominational church membership and fundamental church leadership as to whether women can be ministers. Notable contention over the issue of ordination of practicing homosexuals, however, occurred in the 1980s within the United Church of Canada, and in the 1990s and early 21st century within the Presbyterian Church USA. Likewise, The Episcopal Church, the American branch of the worldwide Anglican Communion, is also divided over the issue of ordination of practicing homosexuals. This conflict has severely damaged relationship between American Anglicans, and their brothers and sisters in the third world, especially Africa and southeast Asia. Tithing will always be an issue in some churches. For the most part, this issue is addressed exclusively by the local church and/or its denomination.

In serving as a minister, people have gone to Reverend Flanigan with all sort of challenges and problems. There is nothing wrong with a person seeking help from a minister. Most ministers provide counseling services to their church members. Reverend Flanigan has offered such services thousand of times over the course of his ministry. He would not provide any specific cases as examples for this book but he dealt with his share of cases involving disloyalty, fairness, integrity, honesty, potential, patience and encouragement.

All of these conditions seem to exist at one time or another in organizations, including the church, even though they may not be always problematic. Whenever human beings interact certain conditions will emerge. Sometimes it is easy to determine whether or not a person is disloyal to the church, other members and/or to the pastor. Others may have observed the persons labeled as disloyal because they have never taken a stand to defend or support any church related activities. The principle of fairness comes form the concept of equity and justice. Reverend Flanigan mentioned that he has observed the fact that children seem to have a good sense of the idea of fairness even though there are differences in how fairness is defined and achieved. Integrity and honesty create the foundation of trust which is important to receiving support from others and long-term personal growth. It is more than just being...it has to be complete or impaired. Potential is the idea that people can grow and develop more and more talents. Of course observation of potential in people, especially within young folks can be evidence in the church. The church has been a platform in many ways for many years for people to develop and improve their God given talents and growth.

In life, there are sequential stages of growth and development. We can learn a lot by watching children grow and develop into responsible adults. As example, the child first learns to turn over on the bed or floor, sit up, crawl, and then walk and run. Each step is essential and each step takes time. Rarely will we notice where a step is skipped. All phases or steps in life's developments are very much the same. Sometimes people will attempt to shortcut the natural process. This is when troubles actually begin. It is true with individuals, with marriages, with families, and with organizations, including churches. The challenge or problem the person faces may have something to do with carrying out an assignment at work, lack of communication with a coworker, or it could be a difference of opinion regarding participation in an event sponsored by the church. The bottom line is, in order to relate effectively with anyone; a wife, a husband, children, friends, neighbors, working associates, or church members, we must learn to listen. Reverend Flanigan feels that listening requires emotional and spiritual strength. Listening involves patience, openness, and a desire to understand something beyond what one already knows. He strongly feels that an answer to all of our challenges and problems can be found in the Holy Bible.

Patience and encouragement are by products of growth and development where they may become more effective through counseling. Reverend Flanigan is intrigued and feel a sense of gratitude when he sees good things happening in the lives of individuals, families, and the church itself that are based on solid principles. He admires the personal strength, maturity and teamwork much greater when it occurs within his own church.

Chapter VII

The Brain and Our Memories

When we started writing this biography, we thought it would be appropriate to discuss memory and follow that by providing an introduction to the brain. However, we discovered through our reading and research that in order to understand memory in mankind, we needed to first, get a clear understanding of the function of the brain. By anybody's measure, if there is no brain there is no memory. A working knowledge of the function of the brain can be obtained from a number of sources. Professional details are beyond the scope of this book. However, the brief review given in the following paragraphs may serve as a helpful tool in making the sections following it more meaningful.

The brain is the most complex thing in the universe. Basically, the brain is a mystery. Scientists and researchers know more about the moon and stars, which are million of miles away, than they know about the brain. There are several reasons why the brain is so mysterious. For one reason, you cannot just open the skull and see how the brain works. It is not like a car where you can raise the hood and watch the engine parts move. If you could open it, you could not play around with it to see how it would respond. Another reason surrounding the mystery of the brain is that the various activities in it function as levels of molecules and atoms, which are very small that cannot be seen by the naked eye. Finally, we must use our brains to ascertain what our brains actually do. We cannot use a machine or computer to explain the brain. The brain is unique. To this day, no one has developed a computer or robot that knows more than the brain.

The one thing scientists and researchers do know is that our imagination, thoughts, memories, and dreams are created and stored inside our brains. We are our brains! The brain is capable of creating space shuttles, inventing new machines, writing books, painting pictures, programming computers, playing the piano, making sand castles, reading a magazine, falling in love, getting jealous, feeling angry, and being overwhelmed by sadness or joy. All of these abilities and emotions mix in our brains to make us the kind of persons we are. A person's brain controls his/her entire body. When we think and remember, we are using our brains to do something very specific. At the same time, the brain is also controlling the person heart so that blood pumps through his/her body. It is telling the person lungs to breathe. It is determining how often the person should blink. It is checking to find out if the person is hungry. It is translating the words the person is reading right now on this page so he/she can understand what he/she can understand what they mean. It is listening to others and the world around him/her. In summary, the brain is doing thousands of things the person do not even think about.

The brain is the primary key element in our memory process. The brain functions similar to a computer whereby it selects, compiles, correlates, and stores all types of information for immediate and long-term future use. I learned in a psychology course that the computer was invented after a through review of the functions of the brain. It was said that the brain functions as the world most powerful and dominant computer. Just as the central control unit of the computer enables it to perform various complex tasks in a rapid fashion, the brain serves as the main part of the nervous system for human and is the center of our thought process. It perceives sensory impulses and regulates both physical and mental motor impulses. It has been proven through study and practice that the human brain is the most important part of the central nervous system. It controls the body and what it does. With the brain we think, remember, and reason. The brain receives such sensations sight, touch, and temperature, and governs the body's reaction to them. Even small injuries to the brain are often serious and may cause death. The human brain is divided into three main parts: the cerebrum, the cerebellum, and the brain stem. The cerebrum is the largest part, overlying all the other parts. It is divided into two halves, call cerebral hemispheres, by a deep fissure. Its surface is smooth, but marked by deep wrinkles or furrows. The outer part of the cerebral hemispheres is made up of gray matter called the cortex. The different regions in the cerebrum are called lobes. The frontal lobes behind the forehead are thought to be the place where the most difficult thinking takes place. It is here that judgment and reasoning develop. Injury to this area changes the personality in most people. If the frontal lobe is cut off from other areas, life can go on but more like that of a lower animal. In the back part of the frontal lobes are the neurons that control voluntary movements of the whole body. There are certain spots for movement of the foot, the face, and hands. Complete injury to even a small area here causes paralysis of the part controlled by those nerve cells. Since the nerve fibers from these motor areas cross before passing through the spinal cord, injury to the right motor area of the brain gives left-sided paralysis. Also, injury to the left motor area paralyzes the right side of the body. The parietal lobes lie on the sides of the brain where they receive sensations of touch, sense of position, pain, and temperature. These centers are connected with the frontal lobes, which recognize whether the sensations are painful or pleasant. The temporal lobes near the ears, have the hearing centers. The occipital lobes in the back have the sense of sight. All of the lobes have what are called association centers where information brought by such sensations as touch, sight, and hearing are related to one another. Memories are formed by these connections. It is because of these associations and memories that we (human) develop our intellect. There is a stronger or dominant side of the cerebrum. In most people the centers of the left side are more highly developed. This makes them right-handed. Left-handed people are equally well developed on the right side of their cerebrum. The second largest part of the brain is the cerebellum. It lies underneath the occipital lobes, or rear part of the cerebrum. The cerebellum has two main activities. It is largely responsible for equilibrium, or sense of balance. Injuries in this section of the brain cause people to stagger and feel dizzy. The cerebellum also has centers that connect with the motor areas of the cerebrum. Its other activity is to co-ordinate motions. By development of the cerebellum, people become more graceful and can perform fine, well-controlled movements. The third part of the brain, known as the brain stem, is located between the cerebrum, cerebellum, and spinal cord. The midbrain forms the uppermost part of the brain stem. The lower part consists of the pons and medulla oblongata. The midbrain forms a way station for the many nerve paths that cross between the cerebrum and the spinal cord. The nerve cells in the hypothalamus control the involuntary nervous system, which regulates secretions, movement of the intestine, or stimulation of the pituitary gland. Reactions to emotions are somehow directed from the hypothalamus. The sleep center is also thought to be located there.

Reviews and discussions of the functions of the brain are important to the understanding how our memories work. However, it does not shed a great amount of light on why people like the Rev. Lud Flanigan have developed and sustained excellent memories. This is one of the primary reasons a large number of people are reading this book. Insights on developing and maintaining a superb memory will be discussed in a later paragraph. Research and practical studies have disclosed that there are several ways how we remember things and certain events. One is by recall. After several days have passed following a group meeting and someone is asked to name the other people who were there, he or she will try to recall their names or what they looked like. Recognition is another way we remember things. As example, if a person is asked if Rudolph Washington attended the meeting, he or she might recognize the name as that of someone who was there. Recall is more difficult to effect than to recognize for most people. If a teacher asks a student to recall what was discussed in class last week it will be more difficult to remember than if the teacher names a subject and asks the student if it had already been discussed. Another way we remember is by images. A person may remember the vacation trip to Florida last summer by having mental pictures of what he saw at the various resorts and/or parks at Disney World. He sees them again and again in his mind's eye. Social scientists call this visual imagery. If a person continue to hear music after he has stopped playing a record, it is called auditory imagery. When someone is said to possess a photographic mind it means that he or she has a high ability to remember by the use of visual imagery. Association is another way of remembering events. Whenever a person has an experience that person usually experiences something else also, either at the same time, just before or just after. These experiences, then, become associated or linked together in his or her thinking. Consequently, when he or she remembers or recognizes one event, it causes him or her to recall the other. Providing accurate directions on how one may find a certain place or location of a business is accomplished through association.

If you have noticed, we have not discussed brain damage. We will not provide an in-depth discussion on brain damage. However, it is important to mention that there are many theories regarding the causes of brain damage. The factors mentioned include the transmission of waves of force, skull deformation, skull vibration, formation of a pressure garolient in the cranial cavity, brain cavitations. No one theory has been generally accepted. Essentially, injuries to the head are caused by a force that is either focal or general or both. All three types of force are serious, but the observations and expectations are slightly different for each one. The types of force may be conceptualized by considering the difference between a moving object that strikes a stationary head and a moving head that strikes a stationary object. The former example involves a focal injury (coup contusion), and the latter example usually involves a generalized injury, a much more profound injury.

The Force of Memory:

There are several dominant forces that are brought to bear as we undertake the various activities of our lives. A superb memory is one of them. A person who possesses an excellent or keen memory attracts a great amount of attention and attains an enormous amount of respect from others. In addition to attention and respect, an excellent memory always pay big dividends from a broader perspective. If you take a moment to reflect upon your school days, you will recall, if you can, that your classmates who always attained the highest grade point average were those who in most instances had a superb memory. A very good memory is similar to wisdom or having large amount of money in the bank. All of us desire an excellent memory.

Even before we explore an in-depth review of the memory and how it actually works, we do know that some people have an exceptional ability to remember other people, things and events. I have made a personal observation about memory. I strongly believe that a better than average memory begins at an early age. I had an opportunity to observe my granddaughter, Courtney from when she was one week old until now…upon the printing of this book. She is now almost four. Courtney's first detection in life was sound. At one week, she was able to distinguish her mother's voice from those of others who talked near her. At two weeks, she begin to watch everything that moved. She observed how people moved their mouths when they were talking or just chewing food. She watched the environment as she was taken from room to room, rides in a car and being introduced to other people. After she had learned to craw, she returned to some of the rooms and other areas she had observed at three months to investigate certain things that captured her attention at that time. At the age of 2, she knew exactly what was in each room and how to find it. At round 3 she was able to recall and pronounce words she had heard at age one. I believe that this transformation occurs within all of us. However, in some people this process of comprehension is more cultivated than others after birth, and especially between the ages of one through 10. This will be discussed in more details under the subject of "Memory Loss."

Webster's New World Dictionary defines memory as the power, act, or process of recalling to mind facts previously learned or past experiences. It is the total of what one remembers. However, in layman terms, memory is the ability to keep in the mind what one has come to know by study or experienced. If it were not for this ability nothing would ever be learned. Everything that happens to a person leaves some kind of mark, trace or record in the brain. This record seems to fade slowly with most people unless it is marked again by a similar act, or by reviewing it, or repeating it. This is what happens when a person memorizes a poem, algebra formula, or anything else.

The classic story of memory is about the man who had gone to the circus as a small boy and returned years later. He was sitting in a cheap seat when an elephant came along, reached up into the stand, wrapped his trunk gently about the man and carried him over to deposit him gently in the best seat in the circus tent. The man turned to his neighbor and said, "The elephant remembered that the last time I was here, years ago, I fed him peanuts." Just then the elephant came back, lifted his trunk, pointed it straight at the man and blew a stream of water in his face. "I forgot I gave them to him in the bag," said the man.

Every time we visit the doctor's office for just about any type of treatment there is an evaluation of our memories. They do not classify it as such but covers it under what is called mental state of a patient. A patient's mental state is evaluated during history-taking. A confused patient is questioned regarding orientation in time and space and is asked to perform simple calculations. Speech disorders may be evaluated by special tests for aphasia, but ability to follow simple commands, to identify, familiar objects, and to read and write indicate that further studies of the speech function are not needed. Memory may be tested by simple questions of personal and general knowledge.

In its most complete form, according to Encyclopedia Britannica, "memory implies a capacity to make use of events and experiences which are treated as belonging to the past life of the person who now describes and uses them." In this fully literal sense, what is remembered can be given a more or less sharply defined position in time and a setting of related events and experiences. Two less complete forms of memory are also generally recognized. In these something belonging to the past life of the person or animal concerned is brought into use again or "repeated," either in a form of words (reciting something learned by heart) or as a style of bodily behavior (carrying out a series of skilled movements). In such cases, as a rule, no specific personal reference is made and no temporal mark is assigned. The second of these two cases, involving the re-employment of learned bodily movements, was called "habit memory" by Henri Bergson, and this descriptive term is often used. It is however misleading, for most instances of skilled movement are not "habits," although they are obviously possible only when there is a basis of earlier learning. All the many views about memory appear to accept, without specifically stating, the fact that whenever and however the past is used over again, it is in attempt to deal with some immediately present situation. Memory is thus based upon earlier perceptual activity and also normally requires some current perceptual activity to set it into operation.

From the earliest speculation about remembering to most of the latest experimentally based views, it is assumed that the critical problems are concerned with how events and experiences can be retained so that they can be reproduced, either in their original mode or with the help of signs and symbols which are regarded as equivalent to that mode. Memory is thus usually considered to function perfectly in proportion to its literal accuracy of reduplication. The ordinary man and the scientist alike generally suppose that when anything happens which affects the behaviour of an organism with a central nervous system, it leaves behind some "trace" or group of traces. I have learned from a personal perspective that every time a memory is made or an activity is learned, it appears that a new connection is made as well. So long as these traces last they can in theory, under appropriate conditions, be restimulated, and then the event or experience which first set them up will be remembered. The experimental psychology of remembering--and all modern experts claim to base their views upon experiment--sets out to discover methods for establishing the requisite conditions for the persistence And length of persistence of traces and for their restimulation.

There have been many studies conducted on the effect of memory. The studies were performed in order to ascertain clues as to how the process actually worked. It was understood many years ago that the brain was the central element in memory but people wanted to know why certain people's memories were superior to others. In 1885, Hermann Ebbinghaus, a German psychologist, introduced two master principles associated with memory. Thus, he was primarily responsible for showing that contrary to beliefs at that time, the methods of science could be applied to the study of the higher thought process. The first principle was that all exact experiment upon mental events must be repeated, under as nearly the same environmental conditions as many be possible, a great number of times. Accidental manifestations will then be canceled out and the statistical uniformities will appear which all material to be used in psychological experiments must be set in a form that is devoid of meaning. If this is not done, the people who are experimented upon will have different initial biases of which nothing, quantitative can be known. Ebbinghaus satisfied his first principle by carrying out protracted experiments on himself. Through this process, he established what was called the "curve of forgetting." It showed that there is a rapidly accelerating early decay of memory during the first 24 hours or so after learning, followed by a very much slower drop, so that what can be remembered after five to ten days shows exceedingly little further that, in the statistical sense, memory for many kinds of meaningful material follows the same general course, thought the initial loss many be less rapid and the subsequent decay more prolonged. In his second principle, Ebbinghaus created the nonsense syllable (three-letter unit in which the middle letter is a vowel, the other two consonants, and which does not form a word) was notable discovery. Following Ebbinghaus' studies, four methods were established on studying memory. These were: 1) the learning method, counting the number of repetitions required for a first correct reproduction of the series used; 2) the saving method, counting the number of repetitions similarly required after known intervals; 3) the prompting method, using imperfect memorization and counting the number of times and places at which prompting is required for perfect recall; and 4) the scoring method, using prescribed intervals after the original presentation, or number of presentations, of the series, then exposing one syllable and requiring recall of another one, the "score" being the proportion of right answer in the whole series.

Encyclopedia Wikipedia provides invaluable information on the function of memory. This information contains enormous facts and insight on understanding the processes and conceptions of memory. In psychology, memory is an organism's mental ability to store, retain and recall information. Traditional studies of memory began in the fields of philosophy, including techniques of artificially enhancing the memory. The late nineteenth and early twentieth century put memory within the paradigms of cognitive psychology. In recent decades, it has become one of the principal pillars of a branch of science called cognitive neuroscience, an interdisciplinary link between cognitive psychology and neuroscience.

In regard to a processing perspective, Wikipedia describes three main stages in the formation and retrieval of memory: 1) Encoding or registration (receiving, processing and combining of received information), 2) Storage (creation of a permanent record of the encoded information) and, 3) Retrieval or recall (calling back the stored information in response to some cue for use in a process or activity)

Sensory memory corresponds approximately to the initial 200-500 milliseconds after an item is perceived. The ability to look at an item, and remember what it looked like with just a second of observation, or memorization, is an example of sensory memory. With very short presentations, participants often report that they seem to see more than they can actually report. The first experiments exploring this form of sensory memory were conducted by George Sperling in 1960 using the "partial report paradigm." Subjects were presented with a grid of 12 letters, arranged into three rows of 4. After a brief presentation, subjects were then played either a high, medium or low tone, cuing them which of the rows to report. Based on these partial report experiments, Sperling was able to show that the capacity of sensory memory was approximately 12 items, but that it degraded very quickly. Because this form of memory degrades so quickly, participants would see the display, but be unable to report all of the items (12 in the "whole report" procedure) before they decayed. This type of memory cannot be prolonged via rehearsal.

Short-term memory allows recall for a period several seconds to a minute without rehearsal. Its capacity is also very limited. In 1956, George A. Miller when working at Bell Laboratories showed through experiments that the store of short term memory was 7 plus or minus 2 items. However, modern estimates of the capacity of short-term memory are lower, typically on the order of 4-5 items, and we know that memory capacity can be increased through a process called chunking. Chunking is a process in which the information (letters and/ or numbers) is rearranged by groups of letters and numbers where people can remember a great deal more than they would if the string was left together. Short-term memory is believed to rely mostly on an acoustic code for storing information, and to a lesser extent a visual code. However, some individuals have been reported to be able to remember large amount of information, quickly, and be able to recall that information in seconds.

Long-term memory is the capacity to store much larger quantities of information for potentially unlimited duration as in sometimes a whole life span. The capacity can also approach infinity or unlimited. For example, given a random seven-digit number, we may remember it for only a few seconds before forgetting, suggesting it was stored in our short-term memory. On the other hand, we can remember telephone numbers for many years through repetition; this information is said to be stored in long-term memory. While short-term memory encodes information acoustically, long-term memory encodes it semantically. This contention was established after showing that test subjects had the least difficult recalling a collection of words that had similar meanings, such as big, large, great, and huge. Short-term memory is supported by transient patterns of neuronal communication, dependent on regions of the frontal lobe and the parietal lobe. Long-term memories, on the other hand, are maintained by more stable and permanent changes in neural connections widely spread throughout the brain. The hippocampus is essential (for learning new information) to the consolidation of information from short-term to long-term memory, although it does not seem to store information itself. Without the hippocampus, new memories are unable to be stored into long-term memory, and there will be a very short attention span. Furthermore, it may be involved in changing neural connections for a period of three months or more after the initial learning. One of the primary functions of sleep is improving consolidation of information, as it can be shown that memory depends on getting sufficient sleep between training and test, and that the hippocampus replays activity from the current day while sleeping.

The classification of memory by specific types has received considerable amount of interest and study. In 1976 J. R. Anderson published an article under "Language, Memory and Thought" where he divided long-term memory into declarative and procedural memories. Declarative memory requires conscious recall, in that some conscious process must call back the information. It is sometimes called explicit memory, since it consists of information that is explicitly stored and retrieved. Declarative memory can be further sub-divided into semantic memory, which concerns facts taken independent of context; episodic memory, which concerns information specific to a particular context, such as a time and place. Semantic memory allows the encoding of abstract knowledge about the world, such as Paris is the capital of France. Episodic memory, on the other hand, is used for more personal memories, such as the sensations, emotions, and personal associations of a particular place or time. Autobiographical memory, memory for particular events within one's own life, is generally viewed as either equivalent to, or a subset of, episodic memory. Visual memory is part of memory preserving some characteristics of our senses pertaining to visual experience. One is able to place in memory information that resembles objects, places, animals or people in sort of a mental image. Visual memory can result in priming and it is assumed some kind of perceptual representational system underlies this phenomenon. In contrast, procedural memory is not based on the conscious recall of information, but on implicit learning. Procedural memory is primarily employed in learning motor skills and should be considered a subset of implicit memory. It is revealed when one does better in a given task due only to repetition, no new explicit memories have been formed, but one is unconsciously accessing aspects of those previous experiences. Procedural memory involved in motor learning depends on the cerebellum and basal ganglia. Topographic memory is the ability to orient oneself in space, to recognize and follow an itinerary, or to recognize familiar places. Getting lost when traveling alone is an example of the failure of topographic memory. This is often reported among elderly patients who are evaluated for dementia. The disorder could be caused by multiple impairments, including difficulties with perception, orientation, and memory.

A further major way to distinguish different memory functions is whether the content to be remembered is in the past, retrospective memory, or whether the content is to be remembered in the future, prospective memory. Thus, retrospective memory as a category includes semantic memory and episodic/autobiographical memory. In contrast, prospective memory is memory for future intentions, or remembering to remember. Prospective memory can be further broken down into event-and-time-based prospective remembering. Time-based prospective memories are triggered by a time-cue, such as going to the doctor at 4pm. Event-based prospective memories are intentions triggered by cues, such as remembering to post a letter after seeing a mailbox. Cues do not need to be related to the action such as the mailbox example, and lists, sticky-notes, knotted handkerchiefs, or string around the finger are all examples of cues that are produced by people as a strategy to enhance prospective memory.

A discussion of memory and its various processes would not be complete without the exploration of memorization itself. Most people can relate to memorization, especially while they were in school where they had to memorize poems and other written material. If you did exceptional well on reciting what you read, you were considered to have a very good memory. On the other hand, if you performed poorly on the test, you were graded as having a less than average memory. I do not recall anybody ever challenging that basis contention. By both definition and practice, memorization is a method of learning that allows an individual to recall information verbatim. Rote learning is the method most often used.

Certain systems in our society are designed in a special way to make it easier for us to memorize desired numbering schemes. However, all organizations working within the same system do not operate on the same wave-link. As example, the state of Alabama has adopted a license plate numbering system that reflects a one slot identification scheme, such as 43J460T. The first two numbers represent that number assigned to each county within the state. The remaining numbers and letters are arranged in such a way that only one vehicle will possess that particular license plate number. The Alabama license plate numbering scheme has been recognized as one of the most difficult systems to remember by people who had a need to remember. A number of states have adopted a much easier system for people to memorize. One such system is used by the state of Louisiana. An example of a license plate used there is JLC 434. Without being given a particular reason, ten people (5 adults & 5 teenagers) were asked which numbering scheme (43J460T or JLC 434) was easier for them to memorize for a later date. All ten respondents selected JLC 434. This type of memorizing or being pitted in a situation to recall a series of numbers and letters lumped together or spaced has important ramifications. In case of a car hit-and-run incident, a person will have only a few seconds to identify and memorize the run-away car. It appears that government officials of the state of Alabama have failed to recognize this critical phenomenon.

Methods of memorizing things have been the subject of much discussion over the years with some writers and researchers using visual alphabets. The spacing effect shows that an individual is more likely to remember a list of items when rehearsal is spaced over an extended period of time. In contrast to this is cramming which is intensive memorization in a short period of time. Cramming is also commonly known in school of study as well. Most students have had experiences in cramming for final exams. Also relevant is the Zeigarnik effect, which states that people remember uncompleted or interrupted tasks better than completed ones. Bluma Zeigarnik, a Soviet psychologist, first studied this phenomenon after her professor noticed that a waiter in a restaurant had better recollections of people who had unpaid orders at the business. The Zeigarnik effect suggests that students who suspend their study, during which they do unrelated activities, such as studying unrelated subjects or playing games, will remember material better than students who complete study sessions without break. Some authors and researchers believe that the paradox of suspense plays a major role in an individual ability to memorize certain events. My experiences in dealing with memorizing certain events and information validate that this fact is basically true. Suspense is a feeling of uncertainty and anxiety about the outcome of certain actions, most often referring to an audience's perceptions in a dramatic work. Suspense is not exclusive to fiction, though. Suspense may operate in any situation where there is a lead up to a big event or dramatic moment, with tension being a primary emotion felt as part of the situation. In suspense movies, the audience experience uncertainty when they expect something bad to happen and have a superior perspective on events in the drama's hierarchy of knowledge, yet they are powerless to do anything about it. Closely related to suspense situations is emotion. Emotion can have a powerful impact on memory. Numerous studies have shown that the most vivid autobiographical memories tend to be of emotional events, which are likely to be recalled more often and with more clarity and detail than neutral events. As example, a person who was involved in an altercation with another over a parking slot at a certain place of business could remember vividly the location, place and date of the event. Still another example would be in a case where you became lost in a certain city on your way to visit a friend or family member. These events stand out in your mind because you were tense during the moments they occurred.

Memory Loss:

The famous Mark Twain once wrote, "I am grown old and my memory is not as active as it used to be. When I was younger I could remember anything, whether it had happened or not; but my faculties are decaying now and soon I shall be so I cannot remember any but the things that never happened. It is sad to go pieces like this, but we all have to do it."

Mark Twain and many others recognized many years ago that our memories served us best during our younger lives. However, memory loss and age do not necessarily go hand and hand. We will learn that there is a difference.

Up to this point in our discussions we have only addressed the brain and our memory process. However, there is such a thing as memory loss in humans. Memory loss is a normal process. As we age, memory lapses become common. It is annoying to forget where we put something like our keys, but it is quite normal. But if a person forget what a key is for or how to use it, he or she may have what doctors call dementia. Serious memory loss is usually identified by a relative or friend. Several factors can cause memory loss. One of the leading factors is depression. Anyone can get depressed, and many of us do during the course of a lifetime. Depression may come on without warning or as a result of a life stress or medical illness or condition. Depression is a complex disorder that has many causes. Genes, imbalances in the chemicals that brain cells use to communicate with each other, hormones, and life experiences are among the factors that play a role. Depression can be hard to recognize, but once it is diagnosed, it can be treated effectively.

Alzheimer's disease is the most common cause of serious memory loss. It is characterized by deposits of a protein (beta-amyloid) in critical areas of the brain. As the disease progresses, the person's memory and judgment declines, and behavioral problems such as wandering and aggression often develop. There are no specific tests for Alzheimer's nor are there any ways to remove beta-amyloid, however, researchers and scientists are working hard on these problems as well as a cure. Another leading cause of severe memory loss is vascular dementia, which develops from blockages in small arteries in the brain. In advanced cases, the memory loss is as severe as in Alzheimer's, but behavioral problems are less likely. Other causes include Lewy body disease, Parkinson's disease, alcohol, and certain infections.

How Can One Improve Memory:

"What the heart has known…it shall never forget." Author: Unknown

There are complicated ways to improve your memory and there are simple ways to do it. In this book, we will describe the simple ways to improve your memory. Before we start, keep in mind that the ideas and methods set forth herein are not guaranteed procedures to produce a superb memory. Some people's abilities to memorize certain things may improve considerably by following these procedures whereas others may not experience any meaningful improvements. However, it is doubtful that one's memory will decline as a direct result of following the practices described here. It all boils down to one basic fact: some people's memories do not need any coaching for improvements. They already have it! People like the Reverent Lud Flanigan who God has blessed to possess and maintain a superb memory need not consider exploring ways to improve their memories.

It is inconclusive that memory may be improved by lifestyle changes such as under taking memory exercises, eating healthily, engaging in moderate physical activity, and reducing stress. One study showed that the consumption of tofu by an elder group caused worse memory retention whereas when tempeh was eaten, the results showed better memory.

Modern psychologists rely on a few principles that can enhance one's memory. The first of these is repetition. Repetition tends to fix associations.

Looking and /or hearing something over and over again is considered the best rule on remembering that particular thing. But repetition is not sufficient. It is necessary to concentrate your attention upon what you are trying to learn. You cannot learn a poem if you are thinking of a football game. Interest in what you are trying to learn is essential. The difference between rote memory and logical memory brings forth several additional principles. Of these, the first is that a good memory depends upon a wise selection of what is worth memorizing. Many people learn too many insignificant details. Selection, thinking, and perspective are as important in memory as in other phases of life. Of two men with an equal array of facts at their command, one may be much more efficient than the other, because he remembers the important and essential, while the other remembers the trivial and insignificant. Perhaps the foremost principle of efficient memorizing is the principle of recall during memorizing. If immediately after reading, the student closes the book and tries to recall what he has read he will find his ability to retain much increased. If you outline what you are learning, run it over in your mind, discuss it with a friend, you will find your memory greatly improved, particularly if the practice is kept up over a period of time when you have a need to remember something.

The International Longevity Center released a report in 2001, which recommended ways for keeping the mind in good functionality until advanced age. Some of the recommendations are to stay intellectually active through learning, training or reading, to keep physically active so to promote blood circulation to the brain, to socialize, to reduce stress, to keep sleep time regular, to avoid depression or emotional instability and to observe good nutrition.

In their book entitled, "The Memory Cure," Thomas H. Crook and Brenda Adderly highly recommend the use of a nutritional supplement called phosphatidylserine (fos-fa-tid-ill-sereen) or PS or improvement in memory. Phosphatidylserine was found through comprehensive research and tests to be by far the best of all drugs and nutritional supplements for treatment in retarding Age-Associated Memory Impairment (AAMI). Dr. Parris M. Kidd, an internationally recognized cell biologist and authority on nutrition and human health, calls PS the 'single best means for conserving memory and other highly brain functions.'

According to Crook and Adderly, PS is most heavily concentrated in the internal layer of the membranes of brain cells. It is directly and actively involved in conducting information across the synaptic gap from one cell to another.

"Small amounts of PS are found in common foods like fish, rice, soy products, and green leafy vegetables which is an essential part of our diet.

However, it is difficult to get enough PS through our food to jump-start the aging cells in our brain," they wrote. To date, more than sixty human studies have been published showing consistently that PS can turn back the clock in the non-diseased aging brain and revitalize its memory functions. In addition, it has been shown that PS can help the individual cope with stress, helps normalize brain biochemistry and physiology at every level, and is safe to take and has no reported adverse effects.

Italian researchers discovered the following after providing (treating) participants with 100 milligram doses of PS with meals three times a day, totally 300 milligrams: 1) Attention, memory , and mood improved, 2) Memory significantly improved, 3) Ability to learn lists of words significantly improved, and 4) PS had lasting effect on cognitive and behavioral functions. PS studies also showed it was beneficial with treatment of Early-stage Alzheimer's patients and those that already had Alzheimer's disease.

The use of PS is the primary element of focus in The Six-Step Memory Cure, set forth by Crook and Adderly. They found that the replacement of PS in supplement form is the most crucial step in halting and reversing age-related memory decline. If a person did nothing else, he or she would almost certainly improve his/her memory or at least halt its decline. However, to obtain the supplement's full effectiveness, they suggested that it should be incorporated into a more complete memory-enhancement program, which will lead to truly dramatic results for most people. The Six-Step Memory Cure Program subscribed by Thomas H. Crook and Brenda Adderly are as follows: 1) Take a PS Supplement daily in the recommended dosage. They suggest that the person begin with 200-300 milligrams daily for 30 days, taking a dose of 100 milligrams twice or three times a day. 2) Exercise your mind to enhance your memory skills, and learn more to enlarge your bank of knowledge from which to draw memories. 3) Protect your health, eat a healthy diet, add PS-boosting supplements. The right diet can optimize energy and ensure sound sleep patterns, making the brain more responsive and mentally alert. A high intake of the primary vitamin antioxidants will help to protect against aging, and its concomitant loss of memory. 4) Change your attitude toward stress. Stress ranks among the world's highest risk factors for bringing on all kinds of health problems. Learning how to handle stressful situations is an important part of the memory cure. We need to emulate the Reverend Lud Flanigan…train ourselves to not worry about anything! 5) Maintain your overall health, and exercise regularly. Your doctor is the one best equipped to deal with memory-related problems, and also can warn a person of more serious problems, such as Alzheimer's disease, or help the person minimize simpler ones such as hearing or visual problems. Researchers in the 1980s found that activity level might be a major culprit in the memory loss of again adults. Consequently, being active and exercising on a regular basis are very important for having a healthy memory. When Reverend Flanigan was asked what were his hobbies, he responded by saying that he spent a lot of his time working in the garden. It was discovered that he still maintains three gardens from early spring until late fall each year. Sometimes he even works in his gardens during the winter months. One of the direct benefits of exercise is that it causes the release of the hormone neurotransmitter or epinephrine, which causes the brain to be more alert and also helps us to maintain a positive mood. 6) Maintain a positive attitude. If you think you can improve your memory, you can do so. Never let yourself down. Always practice the approach that you can do anything positive to promote your own life...and exercise and a positive attitude are just two of them.

Conclusions About Memory:

There are different kinds of spiritual gifts, but the same Sprit gives them. There are different ways of serving, but the same Lord is served. There are different abilities to perform service, but the same God gives ability to everyone for their particular service. I Corinthians 12.4-6

Now we know! The above information collected on memory and its process provided invaluable insight on its functions. However, we know that God has blessed special people like the Reverend Lud Flanigan to possess an exceptional memory. But first, let us revisit what we have learned about memory in our research. Memory is an organism's mental ability to store, retain and recall information. In order to remember something, we must first be exposed to that particular thing. The primary key element to memory in man is the brain. As with the computer, the brain functions as the "central control unit" for the entire body. As discussed previously, the brain encodes or register information, stores it temporarily or permanently, and retrieves or recalls it when requested. Our findings showed that when something is repeated several times, it enhances one's ability to remember it much better. But what about instances where something cannot be repeated? This is where the difference between those who have a superb or better than average memory and those who do not. The so-called "curve of forgetting" takes over in cases of those who have less than a very good memory. It is common knowledge that as we age our abilities to remember decay. Why is this so? As previously stated, this is a normal process in human and other animals.

Memory is a mental faculty which occurs naturally, but which can also be improved. There is a constant stream of books and courses on how to develop or improve a better memory. As the world has developed, humans have had to remember more with each passing generation, but students of physiology insist that the capacity of the human brain to retain information is far greater than what we currently use. Remembering is easier when what we are trying to memorize or store away in our minds is related to something we already know; consequently, many memory methods urge that we try to associate something new with something we know very well. But we found in our research that this fact is not necessary true for everyone. Some people has the God given ability to remember things without efforts to do so. Memory is not always a conscious process. We all have memories that come to mind seemingly by themselves, sometime even unwelcome ones.

All of the above information about the brain and memory process can now allow us to make an official layman's judgment on the force of memory in mankind. A vast majority of the people we meet from time to time who possess a superb memory were God given or born with this gift or talent. The few others attained a good memory through some defined developmental process.

Chapter VIII

Longevity, Aging and Memory

"There is nothing that keeps its youth. So far as I know, but a tree and truth."
Oliver Wendell Holmes

Living a long life has been a subject of discussion and study throughout the history of mankind. In addition to the above statement, Oliver Wendell Holmes also wrote, "youth longs and manhood strives, but age remembers." And on his 91st birthday, March 8, 1932, he told friends, "The riders in a race do not stop short when they reach the goal. There is a little finishing canter before coming to a standstill. There is time to hear the kind voices of friends and to say to one's self, 'the work is done.'"

On January 27, 1759, Samuel Johnson stated, "Whoever lives long must outlive those whom he loves and honors. Such is the condition of our present existence, that life must one time lose its associations, and every inhabitant of the earth must walk downward to the grave alone and unregarded, without any partner of his joy or grief, without any interested witness of his misfortunes or success."

On his 83rd birthday, May 6, 1971, U.S. Representative Emanuel Celler of New York was asked, "How do you grow old so easily?" He replied, "Very easily. I give all my time to it."

Shortly after Justice John Paul Stevens was appointed to the U.S. Supreme Court in 1975, he asked a clerk to ascertain the average age justices retired. He had the study made so that he could plan ahead and retire at that age. The average age was determined to be slightly over 70. In April 2010 Justice Stevens will be 90 years old. If lived until then and remained on the bench, he will become the fifth-longest-serving justice in history.

When a person passes the age of 60, we hear words such as longevity and aging. What is longevity? According to Columbia Encyclopedia, the word longevity denotes the length or duration of the life of an animal or plant, often used to indicate an unusually long life. Encyclopedia Wikipedia states that longevity is sometimes used as a synonym for "life expectancy" in demography. However, this is not the most popular or accepted definition. For the general public as well as writers, the word generally connotes "long life," especially when it concerns someone or something lasting longer than expected. Reflections on longevity have usually gone beyond acknowledging the brevity of human life and have included thinking about methods to extend life. Longevity has been a topic not only for the scientific community but also for writers of travel, science fiction, and utopian novels.

The average human lifespan of threescore and ten years cited in the Bible has been attained only in recent years in areas of the world where man has been largely freed from disease and social and economic disadvantages. In the period around the American Revolution, the average lifespan was less than 35 years. By 1920, in the United States, the average life span had risen to 54 years; and by 1992, the median life span was 75.8 years. Study after study indicate that females are likely to live longer than males.

Life expectancy is continuing to increase for Americans as well as others throughout the world. The fastest growing segment of the population is the 85-and-older age group. The average age of the world's population is increasing at an unprecedented rate. The number of people worldwide age 65 and older is estimated at 506 million as of midyear 2008; by 2040, that number will hit 1.3 billion. Thus, in just over 30 years, the proportion of older people will double from 7 percent to 14 percent of the total world population, according to a report published in early 2009. Within 10 years, for the first time in human history there will be more people aged 65 and older than children under 5 in the world.

There are many difficulties in authenticating the longest human lifespan ever by modern verification standards, due to inaccurate or incomplete birth statistics. Fiction, legend, and folklore have proposed or claimed life spans in the past or future vastly longer than those verified by modern standards, and longevity narratives and unverified longevity claims frequently speak of their existence in the present.

Longevity stories have been around for a long time. These stories include sincere beliefs of claims of extreme age as well as sincerely and insincerely exaggerated claims of extreme age. Each category of belief is based on a different motivation for claiming exceptional age. Some of these claims were religion based whereas others were just made up by different people.

There was a claim for example that if a person followed a certain philosophy or practice, he or she would live to an extreme age (in most cases over 100 years). I recall on an occasion while growing up in my neighborhood I heard a neighbor up the street say he thinks that an elderly lady who lived next to him was at least 95 years old because she was an old lady when he was in the first grade. He was 72 years old himself at the time. Then there are suggestions for people who are seeking extreme longevity need to move to certain parts of the USA or to certain other places in the world because people in these places live to be over 100 years old. There are many who strongly believe that longevity is only enhanced by race-based or family-based factors. To some degree, but certainly not the only factor, it is true that race and/or family relation plays an important role in longevity. It has been stated in other sections of this book that genetic factors are known to influence longevity.

The Gerontology Research Group validates current longevity records by modern standards, and maintains a list of super centenarians; many other invalidated longevity claims exist. Record-holding individuals include: Jeanne Calment (1975-1997, 122 years, 164 days): the oldest person in history whose age has been verified by modern documentation. This defines the modern human lifespan, which is set by the oldest documented individual who ever lived. Shigechiyo Izumi (1865-1986, 120 years, 237 days, disputed): the oldest male ever recognized by the Guinness Book of World Records; this is questioned by some scholars, who believe that conflation of dates or names has compromised the authenticity of Izumi's age. Christian Mortensen (1882-1998, 115 years, 252 days): the oldest male with undisputed modern documentation.

Further review showed that all of the above individuals had virtually lost their abilities to remember events that occurred the day before. In most instances the individuals could not remember their close relatives or friends by the time they reached age 65. In all three cases none of them could find their way to the bathroom.

Despite advancements in medicine, technology, nutrition and lifestyles, most people will not live to be 90 years old. Facts and figures hold these truths to be self-evidence. Not surprisingly, various factors contribute to an individual's longevity. Significant factors in life expectancy include gender, genetics access to health care, hygiene, diet and nutrition, exercise, lifestyle, and crime rates.

Population longevities can be seen as increasing due to increases in life expectancies around the world. The CIA World Factbook provided the following figures for modern countries for 2002 and 2005 (latest figures available):

Country	Years in 2002	Years in 2005
Spain	81.02	82.31
Australia	80.00	80.39
Italy	79.25	79.68
France	79.05	79.60
Germany	77.78	78.65
UK	77.99	78.40
USA	77.40	77.70

The U.S. Census Bureau view on the future of longevity is that life expectancy in the United States will be in the mid-80s by 2050

(Up from 77.85 in 2006) and will top out eventually in the low 90s, baring major scientific advances that can change the rate of human aging itself, as opposed to merely treating the effects of aging as is done today. The Census Bureau also predicted that the United States would have 5.3 million people aged over 100 in 2100. The United Nations has also made projections far out into the future, up to 2300, at which point it projects that life expectancies in most developed countries will be between 100 and 106 years and still rising, though more and more slowly than before. These projections also suggest that life expectancies in poor countries will still be less than those in rich countries in 2300, in some cases by as much as 20 years. The UN itself mentioned that gaps in life expectancy so far in the future may likely not exist, especially since the exchange of technology between rich and poor countries have already been converging over the last 60 years as better medicine, technology, and living conditions became accessible to many people in poor countries. The UN has warned that these projections are uncertain, and caution that any change or advancement in medical technology could invalidate their projections.

Caution is advised because recent increases in the rates of lifestyle diseases, such as obesity, diabetes, hypertension, and heart disease, may drastically slow or reverse this trend toward increasing life expectancy in the developed world. All four have a dramatic impact on life expectancy.

Overweight is often used interchangeably with pre-obese and is generally defined as having more body fat than is optimally healthy. Being overweight is a common condition, especially where food supplies are plentiful and lifestyles are sedentary. As much as 64 percent of the United States adult population is considered either overweight or obese, and this percentage has increased over the last four decades. Excess weight has reached epidemic proportions globally, with more than 1 billion adults being either overweight or obese. Increases have been observed across all age groups.

The odds are very high that you or someone you know has diabetes already or is at risk of developing this disease. Diabetes (medically known as diabetes mellitus) is a chronic metabolic disorder characterized by elevated levels of blood glucose, or sugar. It occurs when the body produces little or no insulin or when the cells do not respond appropriately to the insulin that is produced. Diabetes usually cannot be cured, but left untreated or poorly managed, it can lead to serious long-term complications, including kidney failure, amputation, and blindness. It also increases one's risk for cardiovascular disease, including heart attack and stroke. The number of Americans with diabetes currently exceeds 20 million, or roughly 1 out of 15 people, and many more are at risk.

Hypertension is a chronic medical condition in which the blood pressure is elevated. It is also referred to as "high blood pressure" or shortened to HT, HTN OR HPN. The word "hypertension," by itself, normally refers to systemic, arterial hypertension. Persistent hypertension is one of the risk factors for strokes, heart attacks, heart failure and arterial aneurysm, and is a leading cause of chronic renal failure. Even moderate elevation of arterial blood pressure leads to shortened life expectancy. It is estimated that nearly one billion people are affected by hypertension worldwide, and this figure is predicted to increase to 1.5 billion by 2025. It is estimated that 43 million people in the United States have hypertension or are taking antihypertensive medication, which is almost 24 percent of the adult population. This proportion changes with race, being higher in Blacks and lower in White and Mexican Americans. It also changes with age. In industrialized countries systolic BP rises throughout life, whereas diastolic BP rises until age 55 to 60 years whereby the greater increase in prevalence of hypertension among the elderly is mainly due to systolic hypertension. Geographic patterns also standout because records show that hypertension is more prevalent in the southeastern United States. Another important factor is gender. Hypertension is more prevalent in men, which is an indicator of lifestyle attributes.

Heart disease or cardiopathy is an umbrella term for a variety for different diseases affecting the heart. There are at least eight types of heart disease. As example, coronary artery disease is a disease of the artery caused by the accumulation of athermanous plaques within the walls of the arteries that supply the myocardium. Angina pectoris or chest pain and myocardial infarction or heart attack are symptoms of and conditions caused by coronary heart disease. As of 2007, heart disease was the leading cause of death in the United Sates.

Aging is a force in life we cannot avoid. With each day, we get older. Aging (as in biology) is defined as cumulative changes in an organism, organ, tissue, or cell leading to a decrease in functional capacity in humans, aging is associated with degenerative changes in the skin, bones, heart, blood vessels, lungs, nerves, and other organs and tissues. Webster's New World Medical Dictionary defines aging as the process of becoming older, a process that is genetically determined and environmentally modulated.

Of all the privileges and restrictions applied to human beings, more have been based on age than anything else. There are age qualifications for various public offices (35 for the Presidency, 30 for the Senate, 25 for the House of Representatives, for example) for marriage, for retirement, for enlistment in the armed forces, driving and for voting. Some of these age requirements or restrictions have changed over the years but some have not. The vote for 18-year olds came after the draft of this age group. Mandatory retirement at 65 was born out of the depression in the 1930s to produce more jobs for younger people. In earlier days (1920s to 1940s), retirement was less of a problem because not as many people lived long enough to retire as today. Today, we have all-volunteer armed forces and mandatory retirement at 65 began to fade in the late 1970s and a few years later were outlawed by age discrimination legislation.

The branch of medicine that deals with the disorders of aging in humans is geriatrics. Many disabilities in old age are caused by or related to the deterioration of the circulatory system, e.g., mental deterioration and disturbances of motor and sensory function are often associated with an insufficient blood supply.

The exact cause of aging is unknown. There has been considerable research into aging as it relates to the overall health of individuals and memory. The current status of the state of research on aging is well beyond the confines of this book as well as this writer. However, it can be said here that research into the aging process has provided enormous amount of information, which shows that genetic factors are known to influence longevity. It is believed that highly reactive substances called free radicals can cause cumulative damage to body cells and tissues, and that aging cells are more susceptible to malignant changes. Genetics is defined as the scientific study of heredity. It pertains to humans and all other organisms. Human genetics is comprised of a number of overlapping fields in the transmission of genes within families and inheritance. A gene is the basic biological unit of heredity. It is a segment of deoxyribonucleic acid (DNA) needed to contribute to a function. According to the official Guidelines for Human Gene Nomenclature, a gene is defined as a DNA segment that contributes to phenotype/function. In the absence of demonstrated function a gene may be characterized by sequence, transcription or homology.

The National Institute on Aging (NIA) leads the federal effort on conducting research on aging and the medical, social and behavioral issues of older people. The organization found in preliminary studies that living to extreme old age is unusual and tends to run in some families. NIA, which is a part of the National Institutes of Health (NIH), has initiated a new study aimed at learning more about the secrets to long healthy life, and their investigators are seeking long-lived families to help study this important question. In mid-October 2009, they were contracting older people to see if they and their families might be eligible and willing to participate in the Long Life Family Study. The study was looking for families with two or more healthy brothers and sisters who have lived to old age and can be interviewed in person.

Despite the fact that there has been creditable research linking longevity to genes makeup and a God given blessing, there is still the notion from others who view longevity as a matter of happenstance. As example, a recent study by authors Ernest Abel and Michael Kruger, suggests that the first letter in a person's name could be linked to his/her longevity. If the person name started with the letter "A" for example, he/she would probably have no cause for concern, but if the person name begins with "D," the authors suggest this letter's symbolic significance could result in the person dying sooner than his or her peers. The authors performed their research at Wayne State University in Detroit, MI and were published in the peer-reviewed journal, "Death Studies," in January 2010.

The study examined more than 10,000 athletes and professionals, focusing specifically on those whose names began A, B, C or D, letters associated with the grading system used in our schools. The researchers suggest that because D is associated with poor academic performance, those with D names are more apt to suffer from lower self-esteem, making them more prone to disease. However, the most concrete finding really is not all that striking. Athletes whose names began with D had a median survival age of 68.1 years, while those with names beginning with letters E to Z, which have no grade correlation, had median survival age of 69.9 years. Although studies have indicated that one's name can play a significant role in one's self-esteem as well as how a person is perceived by others, the outcome does not suggest that the letter of a person name is the dominant factor in determining longevity. One reader of the study probably put the results in proper perspectives by writing, "If the initial D is prone to a shorter lifespan because of some psychological association with poor grade then wouldn't the initial F have an even shorter lifespan? Yet this study claims E-Z live longer. The longer lifespan would include F for Failure as well as put a big hole in their supposed theory."

There have been many genuine documented advances in healthcare, however, many elderly people have chronic, incurable progressive diseases and need assistance with the activities of daily living. The greatest challenge facing us as we age is the prevention of physical disability and the extension of active life expectancy. However, the rate of functional limitations among people age 65 and older has declined in recent years. As we age it seems that all types of illnesses are ganging up on us. One of the most noticeable challenges that older people face if they are in good health otherwise is their ability to remember things or having a normal memory process.

It was stated in an earlier section of this book that the Reverend Lud Flanigan was more defined by his ability to remember people and past events than anything else. On November 28, 2009, Reverend Flanigan became 90 years old. By all accounts, it appears that the aging process has not had any detrimental affect on his memory. Since the process of aging brings with it a number of chronic, physical and mental disabilities, his superb memory defies all logical reasoning on this phenomenon.

CHAPTER IX

The History of Mansfield, Louisiana

After discussing the Reverend Lud Flanigan's memory attributes, it is relevant that we review the history of his birthplace, Mansfield and DeSoto Parish, Louisiana. He lived in a few other places; however, Mansfield is the place where he has spent a majority of his life.

An accurate account of the history of Mansfield cannot be told without first providing an overview of DeSoto Parish. The parish is named for Hernando de Soto, the Spaniard who explored the future southeastern United States and discovered and named the Mississippi River. Currently, DeSoto Parish is one of 64 parishes in the state of Louisiana. Until Hernando de Soto's 1542 expedition led him through the area adjacent to land that would become DeSoto Parish, only Indian tribes had traversed this verdant country, and therefore, there is no recorded history. It was not long after this exploration that Pere Olvis and other Catholic priests began visiting the Indians along the Red River. On March 13, 1682, the explorer LaSalle claimed, in the name of France, all the land drained by the Mississippi River and its tributaries. This area included about half of what is now DeSoto Parish. After the Louisiana Purchase in 1803 the land that is now DeSoto Parish was a neutral strip and remained so after the Sabine River became the western boundary between the United States and the Republic of Texas. Communities began to develop in the early 1820's. The first area to be developed was Cow Pens and followed by Screamerville. About 1830 Logansport was established on the bluffs of the Sabine and for a time it was a thriving port, but its importance waned as other Louisiana and Texas towns came into being. It was in 1834 that Thomas Abington settled on the west bank of the Bayou Grand Cane, and Wright D. Hobgood who chose to make his home on the east bank joined him the next year. In 1835, the United States bought the land that is now DeSoto Parish from the Caddo Indians. Forty thousand dollars in cash or goods was to be paid in one year's time with ten thousand dollars to be paid annually for the next four years. According to records that are maintained by the DeSoto Parish Chamber of Commerce, DeSoto Parish was created by Legislative Act 88 of 1843 from the adjacent parishes of Natchitoches and Caddo with some realignment with Sabine Parish, which was established at essentially the same time. The selection of the site for the parish government was also set forth in the legislative action of 1843. The DeSoto Parish Police Jury purchased the site from John Gamble and Charles Edwards on June 5, 1843 for $200.47. Naming of the town was settled when Thomas Abington of Screamerville suggested Mansfield as the name in honor of an English Lord, Chief Justice Mansfield. The first courthouse, a small log structure, was built in 1843 and is now a site maintained by the DeSoto Parish Historical Society. The current courthouse was erected in 1911. It has recently been renovated, and during this procedure stained skylights and other decorative details were rediscovered. The style is a mixture of Mediterranean and English, and is most impressive with arched windows and ionic columns. The structure was placed on National Register of Historic Places in January 1987. It is located in a square of Washington, Texas, Adams, and Franklin Streets. The first jail was built in 1844. The parish seat, Mansfield, was incorporated in 1847.

The first women's college west of the Mississippi River, Mansfield Female College, was founded by the Methodist Church there in 1855. A two-year college, its first class graduated in 1856. Financial difficulties and the threat of war closed the college from 1860 to the end of the American Civil War, during which its buildings served as a hospital for soldiers wounded in the battle of Mansfield; it reopened in 1865. In 1930, Mansfield Female College merged with Centenary College of Louisiana in Shreveport and closed its doors permanently. In 2003, the Louisiana State Legislature moved to convert the main building of Mansfield Female College, the Lyceum, into a future museum.

It was near Mansfield that the great Battle of Mansfield took place on April 8, 1864. This is recognized as the last major victory of the Confederate States of America in the war between the States. History books state that Texans stood with their Louisiana kinsman to preserve Shreveport Louisiana's state capital and save Texas from capture. The Mansfield State Historical Site and also called Mansfield Battlepark is located four miles south of Mansfield on LA 175, situated on a 177-acre area. The museum exhibits Civil War items including weapons, uniforms, letters, diaries, and many other items related to the battle. There is an interpretive trail named in honor of General Mouton, which winds through the grounds. The site was placed on the National Register of Historic Places in 1973.

Mansfield and DeSoto Parish area have experienced considerable growth following the war. Contributing to the growth of Mansfield was King Cotton and later the great lumber mills and the 1912 oil boom in the Naborton oil field. The foundry now known as Hendrix Manufacturing, Nabors Trailers and more recently International Paper Mill and Cleco-Swepco lignite power plant along with timber and cattle and now, the recent discovery of the Haynesville Shale natural gas plant have contributed to further growth.

The city of Mansfield is a participating member of the DeSoto Parish Chamber of Commerce where it describes the area's construction, employment, and sales are currently at their highest level in years. The Louisiana Department of Labor reports an unemployment drop of nearly two percent over the past four years. The area continues to have a thriving timber industry promoted by several major employers that include International Paper Company, a one-half billion dollar paper mill, which employs over 420 people; Louisiana Pacific Corporation, which manufactures plywood; Mims Lumber; and B.R. Bedsole Timber Corporation. Other major employers in the area not previously mentioned include Acme Tube Inc. of Louisiana, DeSoto Regional Health System, DeSoto Parish School Board, which employs more than 650 people, and lignite mining by Dolet Hills Mining Venture. Financial resources have also increased in the area where there are 12 full service financial offices representing 6 institutions. These include community banks, regional banks and credit unions conveniently located to serve the needs of customers.

The Chamber of Commerce states that industrial development is currently progressing at an acceptable pace. Hundreds of acres are available for industry in Mansfield and throughout the DeSoto Parish, especially at the DeSoto Parish Air Industrial Park near Mansfield, Logansport Industrial Park and the I-49 Business Park located at the intersection of Highway 175 and I-49. The 2002 Economic Census showed there were 425 firms or businesses in the city of Mansfield. Of this total, 204 were female owned firms. Shopping opportunities for families and businesses have improved recently. This is supported by the present of shopping malls, antique stores and major discount stores in Mansfield and surrounding areas. I-49 has made it easier to drive to Shreveport for extended shopping and other purposes. The health care industry has experienced growth over the past several years as well. The DeSoto Regional Health Systems in Mansfield has a general medical center and two outpatient clinics under its management. The two clinics are DeSoto Regional Family Medicine located in Logansport and the DeSoto Regional Family Medicine provides outpatient services in Mansfield.

In 2001 a new ambulatory care wing was added to the DeSoto Regional Hospital. The 23,000 square foot structure brought state of the art facilities for emergency care, surgery, radiology and laboratory services. The area is also home for two nursing homes with a total bed capacity of 235. The DeSoto Parish Chamber of Commerce describes housing in Mansfield and within the parish as, "distinct, diverse and delightful. Add the word 'beautiful' to the description of this southern parish. The hundreds of acres of towering pines, enchanting cypress, dogwoods and magnolias make a perfect setting for a comfortable and relaxed lifestyle. The entire area combines the convenience of a big city and the hospitality of a small town with affordable housing and a moderate cost of living. The options for housing are plentiful, from nice subdivisions, patio homes, lakefront homes, to apartments and condos. Many homes in the area date back to the 1800's and early 1900's with many large and stately structures restored and livable. There is a unique blend of housing styles and income levels in every township in the parish. A $75,000 homestead exemption in Louisiana plus very reasonable property taxes are great incentives for home buyers."

According to the U.S. Census Bureau, the city of Mansfield total population for the 2000 census was 5,582 (45.2% male and 54.8 female). Of this total, the racial makeup of the city were 34.1 percent White and 64.3 percent Black or African-Americans. The remaining 1.6 percent was of Hispanic or Latino, American Indian and Alaska Native and Asian races. The median age for the total population was 34.9%; under 5 years of age was 7.3%; 18 years and over was 70.4% and 65 years and over was 16.9%. The social and economic characteristics showed 65.2% of the population was high school graduate or higher and 51.8% (16 years and over) were in the labor force or working in a job. Of those who were 16 years and over, 66.1% worked for a private for-profit organization for wage or salary; 5.5% worked for a private not-for-profit for a wage or salary; 10.3% worked for a local government; 11.4% worked for the state government; 2.5% worked for the federal government; and 3.7% were self-employed. The percentage distribution by occupation in 2000 showed: 22.8% in management, professional and related occupations; 19.2% in service; 21.2% in sales and office; 0.8% in farming, fishing and forestry; 12.5% in construction, extraction, and maintenance; and, 23.6% in production, transportation, and material moving.

The film, The Great Debaters was partially shot in Mansfield and released on December 25, 2007. The story line involves a 1930s debate team from Marshall, Texas. The downtown scenes of Marshall, however, were actually shot on location in downtown Mansfield. The film stars Denzel Washington and Forest Whitaker and was nominated for a Golden Globe award in 2008.

In April 2002, Curtis W. McCoy was elected Mayor of the city of Mansfield. He is a native of the city and is the first African-American to be elected mayor of the city. Mr. McCoy is featured in the "Reflections of Greatness and Spotlights on Legacy" section. He is currently serving a second term and is considering running for a third term for the office in June 2010.

CHAPTER X

DeSoto Parish Public School For African-Americans: History

The genesis of the public education system in the United States can be traced back to its development from its roots in religious schools or the church in the 1600s. Numerous positive changes occurred in the school system between the 1600s and the 1900s, culminating in today's highly decentralized system. The national system of formal education in the United States was developed in the 19th century. It has been recognized that Thomas Jefferson was the first American leader to suggest creating a public school system. His ideas were used in the creation of the first public school system enacted by the U.S. Congress. Today, American public education is primarily the responsibility of the states and individual school districts within each state.

History shows that throughout the 1800s a majority of Louisianans could not afford formal education or were excluded from schools because they were black or Indian. Like most people in the eighteenth century, they could not read or write and signed documents with their mark. Whites, slaves, and free persons of color in colonial Louisiana acquired skills by learning from others, sometimes through formal apprenticeship arrangements.

Louisiana's first public school system was launched in New Orleans in 1841. From this first effort, public education spread throughout Louisiana, but very slowly and sporadically. By the time the Civil War began few parishes in Louisiana had public school.

The model for Louisiana's public school system was that of Massachusetts, which incorporated the plans of education reformer Horace Mann. Many of the early administrators and teachers in Crescent City schools were from

New England. In 1855 the city opened its first normal, or teacher-training, school.

Development of the public education system in DeSoto Parish was to a large degree similar to those created throughout the state and nation. However, there were some regional differences. The operation of the DeSoto Parish school system for Blacks closely paralleled those in other southern school districts. From its creation in the early 1900s until the late 1970s, DeSoto Parish school system functioned as a two-prone system, one for white and another for (African American) Black. Some called it a "separate but equal" system.

According to the history of public education in the U.S., until the 1840s the education system was highly localized and available only to wealthy people. However, reformers wanted all children to gain the benefits of education and took the educational issues to the public. They started publication of the Common School Journal, which strongly argued their case for change. Their case was promoted on the belief that common schooling could create good citizens, unite society and prevent crime and poverty. As a result of their efforts, free public education at the elementary level was made available for all American children in the early 1900s.

Although there were provisions for free public education for children at the elementary level, some of them took advantage of this opportunity whereas many others, especially Blacks did not attend school of any sort. Consequently, all states begin to enact laws requiring children to attend at least elementary school.

Reverend Flanigan recalled the early history of how the church operated its school system. Funding for operation of the school came primarily from the Louisiana Baptist Association. A church had to be a member of the Baptist Association in order to received funding support for the school. He mentioned that W. B. Purvis was a ranking official within the Northwest Association. He further stated that each church contributed ten percent of its intake toward the operation of the church schools during this period. These events take us back from the late 1930s to the late 1950s, more than 60 years ago.

Research findings show that among the Baptist state organizations, none labors harder for the religious and educational uplift of the people than the Northwest No. 2. It was among the oldest associations in the state, and was organized in 1873. The history of the Northwest Association No. 2 indicates that W. B. Purvis at one time served as the association's secretary and that the Mansfield Colored School was owned by this body.

There was scant printed history of public education for African-Americans in DeSoto Parish prior to 1994. Prior to retirement in 1928, the first Principal, DeWitt Johnson had a strong desire to write a history of the school but he did not have the required time to accomplish this task. Printed under the title, "The Original Publication of The School Reunion Committee" for a reunion of all classes in June 1994, was the first ever document released for public use to reflect the history of public education for African-Americans in DeSoto Parish. The manuscript and publication of this document were spearheaded by Louis Flanigan serving in the role as editor. His research, formulation and editing of the information prior to publication required several months of collections and coordination with others before the booklet could be published. The history of DeSoto Parish School System for African-Americans discussed on these pages was taken from the above mentioned document.

According to the above document, the very beginning of public education for African-Americans in DeSoto Parish took place in 1913. The records show that a white frame building consisting of two rooms with each measuring 29 feet by 17 feet was constructed in a piney-wood area in East Mansfield, north of Old Jefferson Highway. The school was given the name of Mansfield Colored School. The name supports an earlier statement indicating that public schools in the south were built and maintained separately because of race. The Mansfield Colored School employed only two faculty members (Mr. Reddix and Mrs. Adams) from its creation in 1913 until early 1915.

DeWitt Johnson, a native of Conroe, Texas and a graduate of Leland College, was appointed to the position of principal of Mansfield Colored School in 1915 after the departure of Mr. Reddix and Mrs. Adams. Mr. Johnson's wife, Elizabeth, a native of Pearlington, Mississippi and also a graduate of Leland College, resigned her position at a small rural school in DeSoto Parish and joined him as an instructor at the school.

During the summer of 1915 before school was scheduled to comments, the Johnsons discovered that improvements to the physical plant had to be made. The improvement task was far greater than what two people could handle. Consequently, they requested help from patrons of the local community where the people responded overwhelmingly in a positive way.

As the knowledge of the school spread, many children throughout the parish were attracted to attend it. The attraction and interest resulted in an increase in enrollment. This created a challenge in that the current space was grossly inadequate as well as additional staff was needed to handle the increase in the student population. Upon realizing that it would be a long and difficult task to accommodate the enlarged enrollment of students and staff help without funds from the school board and state, the Johnsons immediately began an organized effort to obtain support from the local community. This effort resulted in the establishment of organizations (The Mothers' Club/The Forceful Parent Teachers, Parent Teachers Association, Board of Trustees) specifically for the purpose of raising money or to provide labor where needed to keep the school in operation and moving forward. The groups accomplished their intended goal. The funds donated by patrons and raised through home sales and events by the organizations were used to rent a room from a local citizen, Mrs. Sophia Williams. She lived across the road (now Old Jefferson Highway) from the school. The enrollment continued to increase and it was necessary for the school officials to rent two additional rooms from Mrs. Williams. Still, another room was rented from the Smith's Grocery Store, located at the corner of Old Jefferson Highway and Shallowhorne Street.

After resolving the lack of space and supplies problem for the school, in early 1916 Principal Johnson recognized another challenge. He determined that there was a need to lengthen the school session to a more satisfactory term. At that time the school term was only three months in duration. After discussing the need with the DeSoto Parish Superintendent, Principal Johnson was informed by the Superintendent, Mr. Houston, that if patrons and friends would raise $100.00 as a supplement to the Board of Education, the school session would be increased to seven or eight months. The plan failed. Mr. Johnson thought the plan failed because the petition drive was circulated during a period outside of the period during cotton picking season between late August and late October.

Records show that Mr. Johnson had written a letter during his first year as the principal of the school to the DeSoto Parish School Board addressing four issues:

"We desire (1) that the school be organized through the first eight grades, (2) a good Domestic Science Department where the girls can be taught economics, cooking and sewing and, (3) Gardening Department where the boys can learn to till the soil in a systematic way. To do this, we are greatly in need of (1) an enlarged building, at least two recitation rooms and, (2) a Domestic Science Classroom. We are trying to accomplish these improvements with the aid of patrons and friends. These we beg of you to provide."

Records do not show that Principal Johnson received a response from the DeSoto Parish School Board regarding the issues he addressed in his letter.

In 1920, the DeSoto Parish School Board was able to secure funds from the Rosenwald Foundation. Mr. Rosenwald, President of Sears Roebuck and Company, decided to donate a great amount of money to southern states to promote building of a good type school building for both Black and white. The buildings that had already been constructed at the Mansfield school provided matching contributions for the Rosenwald building fund.

The Mansfield Colored School was renamed in 1925 as the DeSoto Parish Training School. Mr. S.M. Shows was Superintendent of the DeSoto Parish schools system. It was noted that Mr. Shows worked exceptional well with Principal DeWitt Johnson and his wife in the operation of the renamed school. It was also noted that the school was organized to train both boys and girls from over the entire parish. Mr. Johnson applied for the provision and the school was approved by the state to train teachers.

In May 1928, the DeSoto Parish Training School held its first graduating class event. Sometime during the same year, Mr. Johnson had a desire to write a history of the school which he and his wife, Elizabeth had developed into a very special educational institution for young African American. Due to the fact that he was very busy managing the school affairs, he was only able to leave fragments of what they had accomplished. He wrote: "Four acres of land and a two room school, granted for a three month period with an attendance of less than fifty pupils was the story of public education for blacks in Mansfield prior to 1915." However, we are sure that if time would have permitted him to do so, he would have documented the expansion of the school to accommodate the increase in enrollment, the additional staff and unwavering support he received from the local community as well as from others.

During the period between 1925 and 1961 the DeSoto Parish Training School enrollment continued to increase and accrued considerable growth in academic achievements. Expansion in the physical plant was also noticeable. Several weeks prior to commencement exercises scheduled for the school on May 17, 1941, Principal DeWitt Johnson wrote the following letter to patrons of the school:

"Dear Patron:

We have added another chapter in the history of education in Mansfield and the parish of DeSoto. On May 16, 1941, when we shall have closed this school year, it will be one of the best we have had under these circumstances. This comes as my second appeal to you for a special contribution to be given during the closing days of our school. As you know, we borrowed $600.00 to buy material used in the completion of this building. We have raised and paid $400.00 ($22.00 interest, making $422.00) leaving a balance of $200.00 that I must raise by the time that school closes. Therefore, I am calling on you. Will you do your beset an d report not later than May 11, our Commencement Sunday? Please save and give $1.00 or more, if possible.

A <u>Good Cause</u> requires much effort. The <u>cause</u> we are engaged in is indeed a <u>Good Cause.</u> I think it is one whose sole purpose is the building of character. The cause

of education is a very <u>outstanding cause.</u> You well know of
the struggle we have had to undergo, and I am proud that
I have had the opportunity to lead in the struggle. I am
sure you are also happy to have had a hand in it...a very
helping hand, too. Without such, we would not have been
so successful.

We have a very beautiful high school building almost
completed. It is modern in every respect, and one for
which you have every reason to be proud. Our entire
plant is in fine shape. So, my friends, Let Us Have A Fine
System. Let Us Leave Nothing Undone. Lest We Hinder
the Progress of Our Children."

DeWitt Johnson retired as Principal of DeSoto Parish Training School in
1947. Oliver P. Baham was appointed as his replacement and served one year
before resigning in 1948. Lee Grant Jacobs was appointed Principal in 1948
and served in that capacity until 1970.

Other (Logansport High, All Saints High, Second Ward High, Third
Ward Elementary, Mansfield Elementary and Johnson Elementary) schools
were built and were successfully maintained in DeSoto Parish during this
period. However, the primary focus in this book is the school (located in
the piney-wood area of East Mansfield where it began as Mansfield Colored
School), renamed as DeSoto Parish Training School in 1925, renamed again
as DeSoto High School in 1962, and finally renamed as DeSoto Jr. High
School in 1979.

It is most significant to mention that during this period under the
tenure of Principal Lee Grant Jacobs (1948 to 1970), in the school's history
that exceptional progresses were made in both academics and athletics
achievements. Prior to the closure of DeSoto High School in May 1979, the Hall
of Honors was filled with certificates, plaques and trophies commemorating
the accomplishments at the school, both individually and collectively. Some
of these accomplishments and honors will be described in the next chapter,
Reflections of Greatness and Spotlights on Legacy.

Currently, there are twelve schools operating under the direction of
DeSoto Parish School Board with the district headquartered in Mansfield:
Pelican All Saints High, Stanley High, Logansport High, Mansfield High,
North DeSoto High, Mansfield Middle, North DeSoto Middle, Logansport
Elementary, Mansfield Elementary 3-5, North DeSoto Elementary 3-5,
Mansfield Elementary PK-2, and North DeSoto Elementary PK-2.

Chapter XI

Notable Alumni and Exemplary Outstanding Team Accomplishments

Achievements: Reflections of Greatness and Spotlights on Legacy

From the day of its inception out of a two-room white frame building and throughout its glorious history, the DeSoto Parish School set aside for African-Americans was a hallmark in developing and preparing young people for successful lives in society. No matter what kind of school or education system a city may have, it seeks to provide recognition for what it regards as achievement. The people of the city of Mansfield and DeSoto Parish do not have to look far to find a school that sets itself apart from all the rest! The school's principals, teachers, parents, and alumni created and sustained an atmosphere designed to inspire success. It is with pride that we count Lud Flanigan among our alumni. What makes us prouder more so is the fact that when he received his certificate after completion of courses of study in 1934, Reverend Flanigan was taking his place in the front of a line of exceptional individuals who followed him, including three sons, Louis, Wilbert, and Roosevelt. Other notable alumni and exemplary outstanding team accomplishments are described in the following paragraphs.

Lee Grant Jacobs, Principal:

DeWitt Johnson is responsible for keeping the doors opened in 1915 for a school building that was created in 1913 with two rooms in the pinewoods of east Mansfield. Lee Grant Jacobs will be remembered as the Principal who rebuilt the school from an old fashion place of teaching and learning into a modern institution of academics as well as athletics dominance. Jacobs should be commended for progress made at the school during the 22-year period he was principal. Success included improved facilities, progress in hiring highly qualified staff, improved academics and increased enrollment every year. Jacobs is responsible for the building of the gymnasium, which is now being leased by the DeSoto High School Alumni Association, Inc. for one dollar a year. The school also made a name for itself in achieving outstanding awards in scholastics each year at the LIALO Rally where DeSoto students always came back with first and second place finishes.

He was a very effective spokesman for the school, a vigorous champion who often visited classrooms, football practices. He was an articulate voice that promoted the school's causes to a wider audience where he went on the road to spread the message to the community at church gatherings and other special events where parents and responsible alumni were in attendant.

Clarence D. Baldwin, Instructor, Coach, Athletic Director:

Few men in any endeavor have brought the kind of success and good character to their endeavors as has coach and athletic director, Baldwin. A graduate of Grambling State University and a former football player under the tutelage of the legendary Eddie Robinson, Baldwin's legacy to athletics is that he was a great coach, a great charter builder, an uncommon man, and a role model par excellence. He created teams of champions at DeSoto and the list of athletics greats he has coached is both long and extensive. Among them, of course, was the great baseball pitcher Vida Blue, who was also a star quarterback for the DeSoto Tigers. Many of Baldwin's great athletes have played college and professional sports. Even more have gone on to become successful citizens in other walks of life. All however, have one thing in common: The desire to be something special, the ambition to be a winner, and the spirit to succeed, all of which was imbedded in them in the classroom and on the football fields and the gymnasiums.

Baldwin is one of the genuine heroes of Mansfield, DeSoto Parish and Louisiana. He has left indelible imprints on the lives of many student-athletes and has complied a record of winning and success that is virtually unmatched in coaching circles. His winning teams gave DeSoto students a sense of pride and achievement and gave the community the feeling of being in a place where success and winning were both commonplace and expected. The great coach rarely disappointed those who had come to expect winning teams from him in either football or basketball. A stern disciplinarian and a smart tactician, he was a coach's coach and a player's coach.

A DeSoto Parish native, Baldwin is one of the few coaches in the history of football in Louisiana to win as many as three consecutive football championships. His teams won championships in 1956, 1957, and 1958. In 1958, against McKinley High School of Baton Rouge, the Tigers scored the most lop-sided victory in the history of championships games in Louisiana, blasting the Baton Rouge team, 58-0. In 26 years as the DeSoto coach, Baldwin won 70 percent of his games, a total of 189 wins. His 1963, DeSoto basketball team also won a state title.

It was Clarence D. Baldwin who helped build DeSoto into a school of champions and who served as the architect of a winning legend that will never be forgotten in Mansfield and by students and supporters of the blue and white Tigers.

Football, DeSoto "Three-Peat" Champions:

Few schools in all of Louisiana's athletic history have dominated or made the most indelible imprint in high school football as did the 1956, 1957, and 1958 DeSoto Tigers. Coached by Clarence D. Baldwin, the Tigers were champions in the LIALO's top classification for three consecutive (1956 to 1958) years. The 1956 team started the run of championship by winning the state title in a 6-6 tie with L.B. Landry of New Orleans in which the game was decided by a single first down. In LIALO play at the time, championship games, which ended in ties, were decided first by first downs and then by penetrations inside an opponent's 10-yard line. This title game was a sterling defensive struggle between the two teams with both teams scoring their touchdowns on back-to-back kickoff returns to start the second half. DeSoto, however, managed to gain the victory when quarterback Louis Flanigan completed a 13-yard pass for a first down to halfback, Willie Houston in the last two minutes of play.

The following year, 1957, DeSoto defeated Capitol High of Baton Rouge, 18-7 to win its second straight title. In 1958, Baldwin's team was one of the greatest to ever play football in Louisiana. The team ran over, around, and through the McKinley High Panthers of Baton Rouge to score the most lopsided win in championship game history. The final score was 58-0. The 1958 team posted a perfect record, peaking in the play-offs with a 169-0 scoring blitz in the last four games. Members of the 1958 team were: Floyd Jenkins, Rudolph Guide, Tommy Dorsey, Fred Johnson Collins, Matthew Sanders, Lloyd West, Wilbert Flanigan, Willie Houston, Lonnie Walker, Freddy Bristo, Tommy Jackson, Floyd Guice, Louis Flanigan, Henry Coleman, Nathaniel Anderson, Alphonse Pea, Mangum Thomas, Curtis Green, Roy Whitaker,

Lowrell Stills, Samuel Pegues, Billy Boyd, Perry Robinson, Robert West, Carlee Riley, Lawrence Atkins, Maxie Boyd and James Bledsoe. Baldwin was assisted in coaching the teams by Coach Willie Robinson.

Basketball, 1963 DeSoto High AAA State Champions:

Championships in the top classification of the now-defunct Louisiana Interscholastic Athletic and Literary Organization (LIALO) were commonplace in football for Coach Clarence D. Baldwin and DeSoto Parish Training and DeSoto High. But while Baldwin was able to fashion numerous basketball teams with fantastic won-loss records, his 1963 team was his first and only team to win the state championship. The win by the 1963 cagers gave Coach Baldwin the distinction of being one of the few coaches in Louisiana to win state championship in football and basketball at the top level of competition in the LIALO. But Baldwin, the consummate coach, had another of his dreams to come through when the 1963 team went "all the way." It was a crowning point for Coach Baldwin's super-successful coaching career and a source of genuine pride for all of the students and people of Mansfield. The 1963 Championship team was led by guard Robert (Pot) Allen, a sure-shooting guard, who had once been Baldwin's athletic manager both in football and basketball and by Charles Johnson, a 6-foot-6 rebounding and defensive specialist. Other team members were Joe Davis, Archie Gilyard, Sammie L. Sharp, Henry Clay, Hilton Crawford, George E. Turner, Johnny Howard, and T.L. Lane. The team was a classic Baldwin squad that played fast break basketball and tough, tough defense.

Willie Houston, Football & Basketball Player:

No former student or supporter of DeSoto Parish Training School has to be reminded of the school's great athletic legacy. DeSoto was a school with a championship attitude with records, trophies, and accomplishments to show for it. The athletic prowess of DeSoto Parish Training School was made larger than life by a bow-legged legend of a football halfback name of Willie Houston, who now makes his home in California. "Special Touchdown" Houston was a legend in his own time and one of the greatest football players ever to play in the state of Louisiana. Houston also played basketball at DeSoto Parish Training School, but he made his mark in football. The human dynamo established records that still stand in Louisiana high school football. In leading the Blue and White Tigers to three state football championships in his four-year high school career, old Number 33, ran 96 touchdowns in an unmatchable career. He scored 19 touchdowns in his freshman season (1955); 26 the next year (1956); 33 in his junior year (1957); and 23 in his senior

(1958). In one game, a Thanksgiving Day game against Charlotte Mitchell of Bossier City, he scored an incredible seven touchdowns. Louis Flanigan, who played quarterback on all of Houston's teams at DeSoto remembers that Houston lost only one football game in high school.

Norvella Goree Whitaker, Instructor, Basketball Coach:

DeSoto Parish Training School accrued one of the proudest wining traditions in high school athletics in the state of Louisiana, and not just in sports for boys. The girls' basketball teams, under the coaching of Norvella Goree Whitaker, also set a standard of winning that is comparable to any school in the state and possibly the entire nation.

Coach Whitaker worked at DeSoto Parish Training School and DeSoto High as a seventh grade Language Arts teacher and basketball coach from September 1954 to January 1970. Her teams won LIALO state championships at the highest level, AAA at the time in 1958, 1964, and 1965. The teams were LIALO AAA state runner-ups in 1962, 1963 and 1966.

Whitaker retired from Stanley High School in 1985 but some of her proudest moments were spent coaching basketball at DeSoto Parish Training School and DeSoto High. Her teams were the premier teams in the state during the 1960s and she, the records will show, was one of the state's highest winning coaches during the era. A graduate of Grambling High and Grambling State University, she earned her Master's degree plus 30 hours at Prairie View A&M. Further study was completed at Tuskegee University, the University of Illinois, and at Northwestern State University. A natural competitor with strong instincts for developing winning teams and instilling character and discipline in young women, Coach Whitaker was one of eight children born to Hosea and Birda Williams Goree of Lincoln Parish Louisiana. She is the widow of the late Culbert Whitaker, II, a native of Holly, LA, and the mother of Juan Hosea Whitaker of the DeSoto High Class of 1978. She is an associate member of the Mt. Moriah Baptist Church.

Clyde Washington, Instructor, Coach:

Clyde Washington was one of the first great football players at DeSoto Parish Training School during the school's fantastic heydays of the 1950s. An offensive lineman, he played the game with ferocity and a commitment that would later earn him an athletic scholarship to Grambling State University where he played on the 1955 Grambling team that went untied and undefeated. For all of his playing days, Washington was a winner, but his winning ways didn't stop there. He also became a winner, first as an assistant coach under the great Clarence Baldwin, and later as a head coach. He coached at DeSoto

High from 1961 to 1979 and later became a head coach at Mansfield High where he fashioned two state championship teams and coached some of the best athletes ever produced in DeSoto Parish. After more than 30 years on the sidelines as an assistant coach and as head coach, Washington retired in 1993, leaving behind him a legacy of teaching and a great tradition of winning. His coaching record will reveal that as a baseball and football coach he produced some stellar athletes, among them baseball pitchers, Vida Blue and Jesse Hudson. Among the star football players he coached as a head coach were Albert Lewis, cornerback, Kansas City Chiefs; Floyd Turner, wide receiver, New Orleans Saints; Glen Hall of the Kansas City Chiefs; and Fred Carter, a college All-American at Alcorn State University.

Catherine Whitaker LeShay, Honorary Student, Entrepreneur:

A 1947 graduate of DeSoto Parish Training School, Catherine Whitaker LeShay has built a proud and impressive record as a successful businessperson in the Mansfield and DeSoto Parish area. A well-liked and prominent citizen of Mansfield, she has been pioneer businessperson in the funeral industry and is one of the area's most successful entrepreneurs. The owner of the Jenkins Funeral Homes in Mansfield and Many, LA, Mrs. LeShay is a respected member of the community who has a wealth of involvement in civic and social affairs.

After graduating from DeSoto Parish Training School, she graduated from Grambling State University with a degree in Elementary Education in 1951. In 1952, she met and married the late George LeShay and they became parents of a daughter, Junear LeShay. In 1963, she became employed as a secretary of the Jenkins Funeral Home under the ownership of the late Robert J. Jenkins and in 1971 received her funeral director's license. In February 1972, she became manager and operator of the business and later acquired ownership of the Jenkins Funeral Home. In 1983,a she remodeled the present day sites of the funeral establishments in both Mansfield and Many, giving any edifice that added both dignity and professionalism for the establishment which would perform funeral ceremonies for many of the area's citizens. As of 2009, she has, through prayer, honesty, caring, and trusts in God served the citizens of the area in their hours of need for more than 37 years.

She is an active member of several religious, civic and social organizations within the community and surrounding areas. These include: Mr. Moriah Baptist Church, Top Ladies of Distinction, 46 and 47 Club, DeSoto and Sabine Parish Chambers of Commerce, Concerned Black Businesses of DeSoto, Inc., Shreveport Local Funeral Directors and Embalmers Associations, National

Funeral Directors and Morticians Association, Associations of Funeral Directors and Embalmers of LA.

C.O. Simpkins, Veteran, Dentist, Civil Rights Leader:

A 1942 graduate of DeSoto Parish Training School, Dr. Simpkins emerged as one of the greatest civil rights leaders and advocates of the people Louisiana has ever known. Born and raised in DeSoto Parish, he became a dentist after serving in the U.S. military and upon setting up his residence and practice in Shreveport, quickly took on the evil system of segregation and racial discrimination that had relegated blacks in Shreveport and North Louisiana to a hapless situation as second class citizens and second class human beings. Having witnessed discrimination and brutal police actions against black citizens growing up in Mansfield, Simpkins said he could no longer stand idly by and watch as his people suffered bias and atrocities uncommon to civilized society.

"I have always believed," he said, "that God didn't make any second class people and I vowed then that I would never be one. I would rather be dead than be treated as a second class human being."

Dr. Simpkins incurred the wrath of segregationists and bigots for his civil rights work in North Louisiana. Racist police officers and members of the Ku Klux Klan and White Citizens Council harassed him, shot at him, placed dead animals with bullet holes through their heads on his lawn. He fought on fearlessly against those who set up against him, never flinching and never looking back, pressing on to bring a full measure of justice, freedom and equality to all African-Americans. He joined with the late Dr. Martin Luther King, Jr. and became a field secretary for the newly formed Southern Christian Leadership Conference. Together with Dr. King, they mapped strategies to attack racism, bigotry and discrimination all over the nation.

Racists set fire to Dr. Simpkins' lakefront home and bombed another of his homes. He received death threats against his family and his medical insurance was cancelled because of the serious jeopardy he stood in. Dr. Simpkins moved to New York and continued to press for freedom, justice and equality for all Americans.

Twenty-seven years after leaving Shreveport, he returned. In 1990 he ran for mayor of the city and lost in a run-off to Hazel Beard. He had finished second in the primary in a field of nine candidates, all but one white. Two years later, he ran successfully for the Louisiana Legislature and won, becoming one of the city's three African-American representatives. He immediately made his presence felt by using laws and budgetary means to change the lot of black people.

Dorothy Howard-Redmond,
Education Advocate, Entrepreneur:

After graduating from DeSoto Parish Training School in 1955, Dorothy Howard-Redmond moved on to personal and business successes. Her training there helped prepare her to become successful, productive and a contributing member of society. First, she started by relocating to Houston, Texas and later moved to Los Angeles, where she currently resides. She is both a thriving entrepreneur and a citizen totally involved in the progress and building of her community. Her love for education and children prompted her to go into the field of childcare. She is owner of three thriving childcare centers, entitled Aloha I, Aloha II, and Aloha III. The centers have over 150 children enrolled and employ more than 18 fulltime staff members. Starting the centers was something of a lifetime dreams a combination of her love for the care and nurturing of children and a desire to give back to the community where she lives.

Howard-Redmond is married to John Redmond, Jr. who is an engineer and inventor. He was self-employed for 25 years, owned an engineering company and holds the patent on airport lighting and landing systems. He also collaborates with members of Congress in the area of minority business enterprise legislation.

Howard-Redmond is prominently involved in a number of social and civic activities in Los Angeles, including work with the Congressional Black Caucus and in the promotion and financing of black students' entry into colleges and universities across the nation. In addition, she is an officer in a childcare consortium dedicated to promoting quality education in young people. As an officer, she shares responsibility for fundraising for scholarships for worthy college students pursuing early childhood education degrees.

Wade Hudson, Author, Publisher:

Wade Hudson has been recognized as one who has achieved success and national prominence after graduating from DeSoto High School. He also graduated from Southern University and has become a nationally prominent author and publisher. His forte is children's books with an emphasis on the African-American experience.

Hudson, who now resides in East Orange, N. J., is president and Chief Executive Officer of Just Us Books, Inc., a company he founded with his wife, Cheryl. The company has gained a national reputation of being one of the most prolific publishers of books and learning materials in the nation. Even with its present success, the company is ticketed for expansion and diversification in the publications market.

One of Hudson's man literary achievements is a book he co-authored called, Afro-Bets. It is a book of black heroes from A to Z. More than 175,000 copies of the book have been printed. He is also the esteemed author of "Jamal's Busy Day" and "Afro-Bets Kids I'm Gonna Be." Another book, "Five Brave Explorers" was released in the fall of 1994.

Hudson has worked as a public relations specialist at Essex County College and Kean College, both located in New Jersey. He is also the author of the children's book, "Beebe's Lonely Saturday" and a children's play entitled "Freedom Star." He has written a number of plays that have been produced on the professional stage, including "Sam Carter Belongs Here," "The Return," "A House Divided," "Black Love Story," and "Dead End."

Hudson's extensive experience in writing and public relations enabled him to become deep involved in the nation's civil rights movement. He has been a field worker for a number of civil rights organizations, including the Congress On Racial Equality (CORE), the Southern Christian Leadership Conference (SCLC) and an organization he founded called the Society for Opportunity, Unity and Leadership (SOUL).

He worked in the music industry, once with a company that gave recording star Madonna her first hit record, "Holiday." Hudson has become a national speaker and serves on the board of numerous cultural book associations. He is the father of a daughter, Katura and a son, Stephan.

Roosevelt Jacobs, Clinical Psychologist, Author:

Doctor Roosevelt Jacobs has distinguished himself in the field of his pursuit. While residing in California, he became one the state's leading clinical psychologist with a wealth of experience, impressive credentials, and professional service and community involvements.

A 1955 graduate of DeSoto Parish Training School, he is a published author in his field and has held numerous high-level professional appointments. He served as a clinical psychologist at the Augustus F. Hawkins Mental Health Center in Los Angeles. He also served as Assistant Professor of the Psychiatric Department at the Charles R. Drew University of Medicine and Science.

After graduating from DeSoto, he earned a Bachelor's degree in Psychology at Pepperdine University in Los Angeles and later earned the Master's degree at the same university. He received the Ph.D. degree from the California School of Professional Psychology in 1975. He has served on the staff of numerous hospitals in Southern California and has worked as Director of the Substance Abuse Counseling Program, College of Allied Health, at Drew University. In 1984, he received the Guy L. Miller, Jr. Award for his work with the university's alcoholism program. His articles on alcoholism, substance abuse, and related subjects have appeared in numerous professional journals. In 1994, he completed writing a manuscript for a book entitled, "The Treatment of Mental Illness in the Hood." Respected as one of the premier authorities on substance abuse, he has appeared regularly as a facilitator and clinicians at numerous seminars and workshops in California and across the nation. Jacobs is married to Ozzie Mae Jacobs and they are the parents of three children.

Cordell Boyd, Film Director, Producer:

The reunion of old grads and alumni members, staff and officials of old DeSoto Parish Training School is the successful brainchild of one of DeSoto Parish Training School most successful and distinguished graduates…Cordell Boyd. Boyd, along with fellow DeSoto Parish Training School graduates Betty Patterson Smith, Cora Patterson Reed, Davidson Jones, Albert Gaston, Pshyra Scott Belle, Calvin Scott, Hazel Mitchell LeBlanc, Johnny B. Pool, Willie Patterson, Billy R. Bradley Green, and Dorothy Howard Green first conceived the reunion idea and nurtured it into the full-bloomed success it has become today. A tremendous debt of gratitude and tribute is owed to these great blue and white Tiger alums for the fellowship, re-acquaintance, and renewed friendship this reunion affords all of us today. They were the founders, who believed in an idea, nurtured its vision, and made it all happen.

After graduating from DeSoto Parish Training School in 1956, Boyd spent four years in the United States Navy and later attended City College of San Francisco. He later worked with the U.S. Postal Service and attended the University of Southern California where he received a degree in Psychology and Political Science. He also attended the Columbia College Media School of Communication where he became certified in the production of television shows and motion pictures.

Boyd scaled numerous professional mountains in his chosen profession as a director lighting for major film projects. His name has appeared on movie and television credits, which have featured the brightest names in show business. With over 20 years in the business, he has been working in lighting for motion pictures such as the widely acclaimed "Portnoy's Complaint," and "The Shootist," which starred John Wayne. In 1982, he worked for the Warner Brothers movie, "The Toy," which featured the acting talents of Richard Pryor and Jackie Gleason. He also worked on the set of the award-winning movie, "Body Guard," which featured Whitney Houston and Kevin Costner. Among his television credits are such hit series as "Gun Smoke," "Storefront Lawyers," and "To Roman With Love,"

Willie Jean Guiton, Teacher, Principal:

Representing a definite link between the old DeSoto Parish Training School and DeSoto Junior High School, Willie J. Guiton did not have to leave the building to maintain the link. A 1959 graduate of DeSoto Parish Training School, Mrs. Willie J. Guiton was principal of DeSoto Junior High School from 1987 to 1994. She began her teaching career in 1962 at Bunnyland Nursery and Kindergarten in Houston, Texas. She began her teaching career in DeSoto Parish in 1981 at Johnson Elementary School and later continued teaching at Mansfield Elementary School and as an adult education teacher in the parish. She holds certification in Elementary Education, Adult Education, Administration and Supervision, and as a Supervisor of Student Teachers.

Guiton graduated from Grambling State University in 1966 with a B.S. degree and later received her Master's degree from Louisiana State University in 1981. She earned the 30-plus Hours at Northwestern State University in 1981.

A certified lay speaker, she is a member of the Shady Grove United Methodist Church and is a chairperson of the church's Christian Education ministry. She is president of the choir and is an assistant Sunday school teacher. She is also vice president of the United Methodist Women's organization. Mrs. Guiton is married to Landry Guiton and they are parents of Cassandra Alexandra, who makes her home in Glendale, CA; LaShonda of Shreveport; and Damonte Guiton of Mansfield.

Lora White Timberlake, Scholar, Distributor, Entrepreneur:

Lora White Timberlake is a native of Mansfield and a member of a prominent family of the city from the late Mr. & Mrs. Thomas L. White, Sr. and Georgie Gilliam White. She is a 1950 graduate of DeSoto Parish Training School, was 'Miss DeSoto' in her senior year and was a magna cum laude graduate of Southern University. A person with an engaging personality and an outstanding high school and college scholar, Lora worked as an educator in Louisiana, Plaquemine and Caddo Parish School systems as Librarian for 30 years, before retiring and taking on the new business of salesmanship.

In 1969 she was awarded the State of Louisiana Modisette Library Award for Walnut Hill School Library. She also received the Shreveport Times and Caddo Education Association "Educator of the Year" award in 1969. Community services include Shreveport Mayor's Women Commission and the Easter Seal Society of Louisiana. She is a member of ALA Sorority.

Seemingly a natural at her new career, she started at the bottom rung as an Amway Products salesperson and worked her way to being a main distributor.

Timberlake represents a new kind of business enterprise and a special kind of business spirit. She has parlayed her business acumen, salesmanship, and a desire to help others into one of the most thriving sales businesses in Louisiana, throughout the U.S. and in some foreign countries. A special representative for Amway Corporation, she is one of the most successful Black Women in North Louisiana and most of her success has come in her second career. She says she has been successful because she has been blessed with a Christian spirit and a desire to be successful and to help others. She says God is the center of whatever she aspires to do and she keeps him central in all of her life and all of her pursuits. A devoted Christian, she also does extensive work with her church and is an accomplished musician who also works in the church music ministry. Further, she says she has been guided all of her life with good family principles and a belief in sharing and caring. She was the wife of the late Marlin L. Timberlake, Sr. and the parents of two children, the late Marlin L. Timberlake, Jr. and Oberon Denise Timberlake Coleman of Houston, Texas. She is also the grandmother of two grandsons.

She has attained numerous awards, gifts, trips, and citations with the company and has, because of her sharing spirit, brought others into the business that have prospered and carved out successful careers for themselves. She has been recognized as one of Amway's top distributors, a position which provides both financial and other personal rewards. She operates her distributorship out of a computer-run warehouse called "The People's Warehouse." She has more than 100 distributors in 16 states, including Alaska and Hawaii, and in five foreign countries (Turkey, Japan, Korea, Saudi Arabia, and Germany).

Curtis W. McCoy, Veteran, Retired Assistant Chief, Police Officer, Entrepreneur, Mayor:

Mr. McCoy is a native of Mansfield, Louisiana. His parents were Vergie Ashton and David McCoy and he was born in September 1948. He had four siblings, one sister, Dicie McCoy Gray and three brothers, Dilliard Ray, Courtlyn Terrell and Brad Williams. He is married to Cassandra Davis McCoy. Mr. McCoy has had three children.

Mayor McCoy is a 1966 graduate of DeSoto High School. He attended Louisiana State University and attained additional training in law enforcement as a patrolman. He is a veteran and served in the United States Army during the Vietnam War era.

Mayor McCoy has an illustrated career as an entrepreneur and public servant. He attained 15 years of experience as a business owner and operator of J & C's Grocery Store located on Johnson Street. Today, he still has ownership to the property. He founded the Mansfield Crime Stoppers organization and is currently a member of the Board of Directors.

He began work with the Mansfield Police Department as a patrolman and moved through the ranks to become Assistant Chief of the department. He retired from the Mansfield Police Department in 1999 and became an officer with the DeSoto Parish Sheriff Office, where he became Captain on the force. In 2000, he retired from DeSoto Parish Sheriff's Office, accumulating 28 years of combined law enforcement services.

Mayor McCoy lost two bids to become DeSoto Parish Sheriff; however, he won the Mansfield mayoralty race by roughly 2 to 1 margin over four term incumbent Harold Cornett in 2002.

Mayor McCoy is a member and deacon of the Saint Luke Missionary Baptist Church in Mansfield where the Reverend Odell Pennywell is pastor. He is currently the president of the Usher Board at the church.

Mayor McCoy has been very successful in all of the endeavors he has pursued after completion of his education at DeSoto High School and we are proud to feature him as, "Reflections of Greatness and Spotlights on Legacy."

Preston Dinkins, College Professor, Military Officer:

Doctor Preston Dinkins is a graduate of DeSoto High School in 1962 and was the class co-valedictorian with Zelma White. His high level of educational achievements did not stop there. He has lived a life consistently with the philosophy that, "It is hard to defeat a man who never gives up." Dr. Dinkins holds a BS degree in Mathematics from Southern University, a MA degree in Mathematics from the University of Oklahoma, a MS degree in Mathematics from Louisiana State University and the PhD degree in (Mathematics) Educational Research from Louisiana State University.

Dr. Dinkins has enjoyed a career in higher education as a mathematics professor and administrator. He has held key positions as an instructor (professor) at the University of Oklahoma, Louisiana State University, Southern University and the United States Army. He served as Professor and Chairperson of the Department of Mathematics at Southern University, Baton Rouge Campus.

Dr. Dinkins completed honorable services in the U.S. Army and is a Vietnam veteran. As a military officer, he served as a U.S. Army Captain. He attended the U.S. Army Air Defense School, the U.S. Army Management School and the Defense Language Institute Support Command. He served as an instructor, a statistician, property book officer, operations research and systems analysis officer, military advisor and an air defense artillery officer. He was conferred the Operations Research and Systems Analysis Executive Course Diploma. He also served as the Head of the Computer Science Department at Ft. Bliss, Texas.

He has expertise in the areas of executive management, creating innovative teaching, property management, statistical analysis, record keeping, recruitment, job placement, professional publications, presentations at professional conferences and grant writing. He has been awarded educational grants in excess of $325,000.

Dr. Dinkins has served on several Board of Directors, including the Baton Rouge Early Risers Kiwanis, City of Baker Heritage Museum, The Greater Baton Rouge Pan-Hellenic Council and The Beta Iota Lambda Foundation of Alpha Phi Alpha, Inc. He is a volunteer for the Louisiana Capital Area Chapter of The American Red Cross and he serves as a board member on the City of Baker Fire and Police Civil Service Board.

Awards and honors that have been presented to Dr. Dinkins include the Distinguish Service Award, National Association of Mathematics; the Faculty Development Award from Southern University; the 100 Black Women Excellence in Teaching Award; Faculty Award for Excellence In Mathematics, Southern University; the National Defense Service Medal, U.S. Army; the Vietnam Services Medal, U.S. Army; the Republic of Vietnam Campaign Medal, U.S. Army; Joint Service Commendation Medal, U.S. Army; Certificate of Appreciation, the U.S. Army; the Phi Delta Kappa KAPPAN of the Year, Southern University Chapter; the Phi Delta Kappa President Award, Southern University Chapter and the Kiwanian of the Year Award, Baton Rouge Early Risers.

Preston is the son of Horace and Myrtis Lee Dinkins. His father is deceased. His mother is alive and recently celebrated her 88th birthday. Dr. Dinkins has one daughter, Erica L. Dinkins, who has a PhD degree in Speech Pathology and Audiology from Louisiana State University.

Freddie C. Henderson, Minister, Religious and Community Leader:

Freddie C. Henderson was born in Mansfield, Louisiana and is the eldest of three sons born to the late Mrs. Ella R. Henderson and Mr. Fred D. Henderson. He graduated from DeSoto High School as an honor student in 1962 and served as the class President that year. Henderson holds a BA degree in Sociology from Wiley College, Marshall, Texas.

Upon completion of College, Henderson matriculated at The Interdenominational Theological Center (Gammon Seminary) in Atlanta, GA receiving a Master of Divinity Degree in 1970. The call to ministry came at an early age and Freddie received Exhorter's license in 1958 at age 12 and served as a student pastor as a senior in High School. During his college years, Henderson served churches in Louisiana, traveling back on weekends to take care of pastoral duties.

Reverend Henderson has served as Director of Financial Aid and Chief Counselor of Upward Bound at Morehouse College, in Atlanta, GA. In 1972, he became Director of The Wesley Foundation Campus Ministry at Southern University in Baton Rouge, LA until 1979 when he was appointed to Jordan United Methodist Church (UMC) in North Baton Rouge where he served until 1988. He has served the United Methodist Church as a pastor in the Baton Rouge area for more than forty years including pastorates at Hartzell, Shiloh, and Lejeune churches. He also has served as a Juvenile Chaplain at The Jetson Correctional Institute in Baker, La.

Reverend Henderson has served on many of the boards and committees at the district, conference, and jurisdictional levels. He was elected as a delegate to the General and Jurisdictional Conferences in the years 1996, 2000, and 2004.

From 1988-1998, Reverend Henderson served as pastor of Wesley United Methodist Church in downtown Baton Rouge where the worship services aired on live radio. The broadcast was number three in the polls for the 11:00 Sunday time slot for the Baton Rouge metro area.

In 1998 Reverend Henderson was appointed Superintendent of the New Orleans District of the Louisiana Conference. The last year was dealing with the devastating storms Katrina and Rita in the summer of 2005 where all of the churches on the district were affected, some of which are still closed.

In June 2006, he was appointed Director of Disaster Preparedness for The Louisiana Annual Conference. This ministry entails building emergency preparedness into the culture of our churches across the annual conference. In June 2009, Reverend Henderson was given the distinction of "Passing the Mantle" to new ordinands at the session of Annual Conference which was held in Kenner, Louisiana. Although officially retired, he has been serving the St. Paul's-St. Luke's Charge in Baton Rouge since June 2009.

His interests include listening to music, sports, reading and "gadgetry." He also has a passion for mentoring the youth and children to hopefully instill awareness in them that they are vital to our continuing challenges of building a better society where all of God's people can live together experiencing Christ's love.

One of the significant aspects of Reverend Henderson's career is that he was serving as Superintendent of The New Orleans District of The Louisiana Conference-United Methodist when hurricanes Katrina and Rita devastated the coast in 2005. That particular district at the time was comprised of churches from Grand Isle and Buras to the Mississippi line on the North, and from Laplace, Covington-Mandeville for a total of eighty churches. Of course, this also included all of Metro New Orleans, Kenner, Metairie, and the West Bank. Upon working with this recovery efforts was a major undertaking for him and which could not have been accomplished without the assistance of thousands from around the globe.

Reverend Henderson was married to Gloria Listach Henderson for 43 years until her transition to eternal rest in September 2009. Three children; sons Freddie Jr. and Nora and daughter Keisha were born to Freddie and Gloria. They are the proud grandparents of eight (8) grandchildren who are sources of joy and bring much delight to their days.

Lloyd D. Jackson, Engineer, Military Officer, Teacher, School Principal, DHSAA Advisor:

An exact and legitimate history of DeSoto Parish Training School and DeSoto High School cannot be told without the inclusion of the late Lloyd D. Jackson in its contents. This book itself, would not be complete without bringing to bear Mr. Jackson's contributions to the school, the community, and his relationship with the Reverend Lud Flanigan.

Lloyd D. Jackson and the Reverend Lud Flanigan were the best of friends. On countless occasions they interacted regarding DeSoto High School, church, civic organizations and community issues to precipitate positive outcomes for other people. Not only did they call each other by their first name, they always shared their favorite jokes whenever they met.

Lloyd Dorsey Jackson was born in Mansfield, Louisiana and was the son of the Reverend Grant Dorsey and Ruth Hazel Sharp Jackson. He received his early and high school education at DeSoto Parish Training School. After graduating from high school, he continued his education at Tuskegee Institute (now Tuskegee University) in Tuskegee, Alabama.

While pursing an advance degree at Tuskegee Institute, he was active in several extracurricular activities which included Omega Psi Phi Fraternity, Business Manager of the Class of 1950, Cadet Colonel of the Infantry Battalion, member of the Honor Guard, Editor of the Yearbook Staff, Art Editor of the Tuskegee Staff, member of the Technical Arts Club and the Chapter Ushers Staff.

Mr. Jackson was most active in the Reserve Officer Training Corp (ROTC), which led to a Regular Army Commission and Distinguished Military Graduate and the rank of 2nd Lieutenant. He graduated from Tuskegee Institute with a B.S. degree in Architecture Engineering and entered into the United States Army at Fort Hood, Texas. He was the Training Aids

Officer of the Post Head Quarters at Ft. Hood. He received Military Orders to report for duty in the Korean War with Company M of 3rd Battalion of the 32nd Infantry Regiment of the Seventh Division. It was at this post where he was awarded the rank of 1st Lieutenant in the United States Infantry. He was the first African-American officer to lead and command an all white platoon in the 32nd Infantry Regiment. He was awarded the Combat Infantry Badge, the Bronze Star Medal, the Good Conduct Medal, the Korean Service Medal, and the United Nation Service Medal decorations.

The career in the United States Army took Mr. Jackson to many places within the nation and throughout the world, to such places as, Fort Hood, Texas; San Francisco, California; Hawaiian Islands; Tokyo, Yokohama, and Sasebo, Japan; Pusan, Incheon, Seoul, Yodonpo, Heartbreak Ridge, Korea; Iron Triangle, Vietnam; and Camp Chaffee, Arkansas.

After his tour of duty in the military, Mr. Jackson continued his education at Southern University in Baton Rouge, LA where he received a B.S. degree in mathematics and social studies. He received a master's degree in chemistry and physics from Miami University, Oxford, OH. He also completed thirty hours of study beyond the master's degree from Northwestern State University, Natchitoches, LA.

Mr. Jackson began his teaching career at his Alma Mater DeSoto High School immediately following his graduation from Southern University. The first subjects he taught at DeSoto High School were mathematics and science and later also taught chemistry and physics. His teaching career at DeSoto High spanned from 1954 through 1970. He was the Principal of DeSoto High School and DeSoto Junior High School from 1970 through 1984. After the closure of DeSoto Junior High in 1984, he became the Coordinator of Special Education for the entire DeSoto Parish and he held this position for ten years. We are most proud to state that Mr. Jackson served DeSoto Parish exceptional well as a teacher of mathematics and sciences for fifteen years, as a Principal for fifteen years, and as a coordinator and supervisor for ten more years, and for a combined total tenure of forty years in education.

Mr. Jackson earned a number of certificates, permits and awards during his lifetime. Some of these include, Child search Coordinator, Grades 1-12; School Superintendent, Grades 1-12; Supervisor of Student Teaching, Grades 1-12; Parish or City School Supervisor, Grades 1-12; Principal, Grades K-12; Chemistry, Grades 6-12; Physics, Grades 6-12; General Science, Grades 6-12; Mathematics, Grades 6-12; and Social Studies, Grades 6-12. He was also awarded the Bellsouth Award for teaching chemistry in DeSoto Parish; the St. John Baptist Church award for outstanding Contribution and Service as their Secretary-Treasurer and was also presented the Kiwanis Club President Award.

As an architect engineer, Mr. Jackson spent his summers designing and building homes and churches in DeSoto Parish. Some of the structures he is responsible for designing are, The Wesley United Parsonage, Cedar Hill Baptist Church, Moore' Chapel Baptist Church, New Morning Glory Baptist, Saint John Baptist Church, Ira Holmes' home, Thomas White, Junior's home, Thomas Spears' home, Grant Jackson's home, Ellen Crump's home and his own personal home.

Mr. Jackson was one of the founders of the DeSoto Parish Teacher's Federal Credit Union and served as President of the organization. He is responsible for organizing the DeSoto High School Alumni Association (DHSAA) and the organization's Chapter 1st President's Award. He served as Commander In Chief of Nehemiah Consistory #56. He was active in Holy Royal Arch Chapter #15, Stars of Prince Hall #241, V.A. Gardner Order of Eastern Star #151, Prosperity Court #6 Heroines of Jericho. He was an active member of the St. John Baptist Church and served in the positions as Church Treasurer, Deacon, member of the Board of Trustees and as a member of the Building and Grounds Committee. He was also active in various community organizations, such as DeSoto High School Alumni Association, where he served as an Adviser for several years, DeSoto Parish Southern University Alumni Association, Kiwanis Club and the United Radio Amateur Club.

Mr. Jackson was married to Frances Marie of Baton Rouge, LA and they had three children; Waymon L. Jackson, Austin, Texas, Worlita Jackson-Williams, Mansfield, LA and Worrick L. Jackson, Beaumont, Texas. They had three grandchildren Alexia Denea, Simone Dakota and Iyanna Marie.

Chapter XII

Emergency Telephone Numbers

Upon the development of the manuscript for this book, a number of references have been made to the Bible. Consequently, it is most appropriate to refer to the Bible in times of special needs. The following listing was obtained from the Westminster Presbyterian Church, Tuskegee, AL newsletter, dated November 16, 2003.

These are more effective than 911
When-

You are sad, phone	John 14
You have sinned, phone	Psalm 51
You are facing danger, phone	Psalm 91
People have failed you, phone	Psalm 27
It feels as though God is far from you, phone	Psalm 139
Your faith needs stimulation, phone	Hebrews 11
You are alone and scared, phone	Psalm 23

You are worried, phone	Matthew 8:19-34
You are hurt and critical, phone	1 Corinthians 13
You wonder about Christianity, phone	2 Corinthians 5:15-18
You feel like an outcast, phone	Romans 8:31-39
You are seeking peace, phone	Matthew 11:25-30
It feels as if the world is bigger than God, phone	Psalm 90
You need Christ like insurance, phone	Romans 8:1-30
You are leaving home for a trip, phone	Psalm 121
You are praying for yourself, phone	Psalm 86
You require courage for a task, phone	Joshua 1
Inflations and investments are bogging your thoughts, phone	Mark 10:17-31
You are depressive, phone	Psalm 27
Your bank account is empty, phone	Psalm 37
You lose faith in mankind, phone	1 Corinthians 13
It looks like people are unfriendly, phone	John 15
You are losing hope, phone	Psalm 126
You feel the world is small compared to you, phone	Psalm 19

You want to carry fruit, phone	John 15
Paul's secret for happiness, phone	Colossians 3:12-17
With big opportunity/discovery, phone	Isaiah 55
To get along with other people, phone	Romans 12
ALTERNATE NUMBERS:	
For dealing with fear, call	Psalm 3:4-7
For security, call	Psalm 121:3
For assurance, call	Mark 8:35
For reassurance, call	Psalm 145:18

ALL OF THESE NUMBERS MAY BE PHONED DIRECTLY. NO OPERATOR ASSISTANCE IS NECESSARY. ALL LINES TO HEAVEN ARE AVAILABLE 24 HOURS A DAY. FEED YOUR FAITH, AND DOUBT WILL STARVE TO DEATH.

References

"Alzheimer's Disease, More than Memory Loss & Normal Aging." Pri-Med Patient Education Center. (Medical Group Management Association, Fort Dodge, IA, 2009)

Baddeley, A. D. (1966). *"The influence of acoustic and Semantic similarity on long-term memory for word sequences."*

Britannica Encyclopedia, (Encyclopedia Britannica, Inc., Ill, 2007)

Byrd, Jerry, *"Jerry Byrd's Football Country."* (Shreveport Publishing Corp., Shreveport, LA, 1981)

Compton's Pictured encyclopedia and Fact-Index, F.E. Compton & Company. (William Benton, Publisher, Chicago, Ill, 2003)

Conrad, R. (1964). *"Acoustic Confusions in Immediate Memory."* British Journal of Psychology.

Crook, Thomas H. III, Ph.D. and Brenda Adderly, M.H.A. *"The Memory Cure."* (Pocket Books, a division of Simon & Schuster Inc., New York, NY, 1998)

DeSoto Parish Chamber of Commerce. (http://www.desotoparishchamber. net/Custom, 2009)

"DeSoto Parish History," Sesquicentennial Edition. (DeSoto Historical and Genealogical Society Mansfield, Louisiana, 1995)

Discover DeSoto. (http://www.discover Desoto.com/attract/index.asp, 2009)

Flanigan, Louis, Cardell Pinkney, Bobby Sewell, Connie Sewell, Doretha Lindsay. *"77ᵗʰ Anniversary of Paradise Baptist Church:"* 1948-1996. (Paradise Baptist Church Publication, 1996)

Flanigan, Louis, Lloyd D. Jackson, Orbidee Ware Norris, Barbara Reed-Hubbard. *"From These Roots The Spirit Lives on: A Reunion of all Classes, Spanning 51 Years: 1928-1979 (DeSoto Parish Training School: 1915-1961; DeSoto High School: 1962-1979), The 1994 Reunion Chronicle."* (The Official Publication of The School Reunion Committee, Mansfield, LA, 1994)

Flanigan, Louis, John Taylor, Claudine Ellis. *"29ᵗʰ Celebration in Appreciation to Pastor Lud Flanigan."* Paradise Baptist Church (Mays Printing Company, Shreveport, LA, 1984)

Gavrilov LA, Gavrilova NS. *"Reliability Theory of Aging and Longevity."* Handbook of the Biology of Aging, 6ᵗʰ Edition. (Academic Press. San Diego, CA, 2006)

Gavrilov La, Gavrilova NS. *"The reliability theory of aging and longevity."* (Journal of Theoretical Biology, Academic Press. San Diego, CA, 2001)

Huso, Deborah. *"Can Your Name Predict Longevity?"* (AOL Health, Healthy Living/Aging-Well, http://www.aolhealth.com, 2010)

Kenner, Cornelia Vanderstaay, Cathie E. Guzzetta, and Barbara Montgomery Dossey. *"Critical Care Nursing: Body, Mind and Spirit."* Second Edition. (Little, Brown and Company, Boston, MA, Toronto, Canada, 1985)

"Memory Loss." Pri-Med Patient Education Center. (Medical Group Management Association. Fort Dodge, IA, 2009)

Newquist, Harvey, *"The Great Brain Book, An Inside Look at The Inside of Your Head."* (Scholastic Inc., New York, NY, 2008)

Speaker's Lifetime Library. Leonard and Thelma Spinrad. (Parker Publishing Company, Inc., West Nyack, New York, 1979)

Suitts, Steve, Southern Education Foundation. *"Crisis of a New Majority: Low-Income Students in The South's Public Schools."* (Southern Spaces. 2008)

Sweeney, Michael S. & Richard Restak, M.D., BRAIN: *"The Complete Mind; How It Develops, How It Works, And How To Keep It Sharp."* (National Geographic, Washington, D.C., 2009)

Thattai, Deeptha, *"A History of Public Education in the United States. Public Education in The United States* (http://www.servintfree.net, 2009)

"The Merck Manual of Diagnosis and Therapy," Twelfth Edition. (Merck Sharp & Dohme Research Laboratories, Merck & Co., Inc., Rahway, N.J., 1972)

The Random House Dictionary of The English Language, Second Edition. (Random House, Inc., New York, NY, 1987)

The World Book Encyclopedia, Fifty Editions. (World Book, Inc., Chicago, Ill, 2009)

U.S. Census Bureau. (http://fact finder.census.gov/servlet/Reference, 2009)

Wiese, Bill, *"23 Minutes in Hell."* (Charisma House, Lake Mary, FL, 2006)

Wikipedia Encyclopedia, Free Encyclopedia. (http://en.Wikipedia.org/wiki/Suspense, 2009)

INDEX

About the Author

Jimmie L. Clay, MHA, FACHE, is a native of Mansfield, Louisiana and a graduate of DeSoto High School of the city. He is a former Veterans Affairs (VA) Healthcare System Director. He retired from VA in 2000 after successfully completing more than 33 years of leadership service. He has a Bachelor of Science degree in Business Administration and Masters degree in Management/Human Relations & Organization Behavior and Healthcare Management. He is responsible for the establishment of a new community based outpatient clinic in south Alabama and for the integration of the Montgomery and Tuskegee VA Medical Centers prior to retirement. Clay received a wide variety of recognitions, awards, and honors not only from VA, but also from many civic, professional, and veterans service organizations. He is a life Fellow in the American College of Healthcare Executives, a professional organization whose mission includes promotion of high ethical standards of conduct. He was a representative for VA on the President's Task Force on National Health Care Reform during the late 1990s and was commented for his performance. Clay is the author of three other books. His latest book, "Never Ask For An Apology" sold more than 4,000 copies.